CHOOSING – AND USING – HYMNS

By the same author:

Church Music in a Changing World (Mowbray)
A Handbook of Parish Music (Mowbray)
Making Church Music Work (Mowbray)
The World of Church Music—Editor (RSCM)
Music and the Alternative Service Book—Editor
(Addington Press—RSCM/Mowbray)
The ASB Psalter and Canticles—Editor (Collins)
Church Music at the Crossroads
(Marshall, Morgan and Scott)
The Psalms—Their use and Performance Today—Editor
(RSCM)
The Church Musician as Conductor (RSCM)

CHOOSING
—AND USING—
HYMNS

by

LIONEL DAKERS

Director of the Royal School of Church Music

MOWBRAY
LONDON & OXFORD

ISBN 0 264 67034 5

First published 1985
by A. R. Mowbray & Co. Ltd,
Saint Thomas House, Becket Street,
Oxford, OX1 1SJ

Typeset by Cotswold Typesetting Ltd, Cheltenham.
Printed and bound in Great Britain by
Cox & Wyman Ltd, Reading

British Library Cataloguing in Publication Data
Dakers, Lionel
Choosing–and using–hymns.–(Mowbray's popular Christian paperbacks)
1. Church of England–Hymns
I. Title
264'.0302 BV370

ISBN 0-264-67034-5

Dedicated to
the trains, planes, airport departure lounges
and hotel bedrooms where, in undisturbed solitude,
most of this book was written.

FOREWORD

Few liturgical experiences can excite the heart more than the singing of a good hymn which is carefully chosen, well played and tunefully sung. When these conditions are not fulfilled, opportunities for enriching worship are squandered.

We live at a time when the writing of hymns is again a fruitful ingredient of church life, enabling those charged with the ordering of worship to bring out of their treasure things both new and old. They will find in this book by the Director of the Royal School of Church Music sound and sensitive guidance based on wide experience.

September 1985 + ROBERT CANTUAR

CONTENTS

Abbreviations used in the text are:

A and M = *Hymns Ancient and Modern*
AMR = *Hymns Ancient and Modern Revised* (1950)
A and M NSE = *Hymns Ancient and Modern New Standard Edition* (1983)
EH = *The English Hymnal*
SP = *Songs of Praise*

1
INTRODUCTION

Setting the scene

Hymns are everyone's music in church. They are inevitable and they are inescapable. Every so many minutes in almost every act of public worship the entire corpus—clergy, choir and congregation alike—are brought together in a joint preoccupation, that of singing a hymn.

Such is the universality of hymnody. In most instances, choirs sing more hymns every Sunday than any other kind of music, but whether they give hymns the same emphasis or the degree of priority they give to the preparation of an anthem is another matter. For many choirs hymns are both a chore and an unwanted necessity, an attitude of mind which is all too obvious from the way in which they are sometimes sung and played. For those of us in the congregation the impact of how the musicians approach and project hymnody is a major factor in the completeness or otherwise of worship.

In a nutshell, the choice and performance of hymns often leaves much to be desired, simply because so many opportunities are missed. Hence, one of the main reasons for this book.

Although I happen to be an Anglican, I am in no way writing exclusively for Anglicans any more than as an Englishman I am directing my thoughts exclusively to those within the United Kingdom. What I have to say has no denominational or geographical boundaries or slant, but is directed towards *all* concerned in worship, be they clergy, musicians, or those frequently long suffering persons in the pews whose ranks I have joined in the past twelve years, an experience which affords me a vantage point which can be as revealing as it can be traumatic

However we worship and whatever our denomination, there must of necessity be a common approach in how we choose and use hymns as much as there is a right and wrong way in which to sing and play them.

Every aspect governing the choice and subsequent performance of hymns is, or should be, a demanding and time consuming exercise. In practice it can be all too perfunctory.

Hymns, as I shall seek to show, can be a most exciting ingredient of worship. Yet, as I hinted just now, they suffer when the musicians off-load them as inconsequential. Time and again we fail to realize just how difficult it is to bring to life what can all too easily be an indigestible succession of block harmonies devoid of rhythm or vitality.

The danger lies to some extent in our thinking of hymns as being very simple, which of course they are on the face of it, and certainly by marked contrast with many other forms of vocal music. Therein also lies the challenge. Most simple music is far less easy to bring off than many a difficult piece.

Some of the challenges

We live in a world inundated to flood level with new hymns. These range, both in words and music, from the predictable cast in a familiar mould to the less familiar and certainly the less traditional, some of which is both bizarre and exotic in the extreme. In many respects there is nothing new in this, for the Victorians were equally prone to pursuing such contrasts. Although *Golden Bells* may be a particularly diabolical and misdirected example (subtitled 'Hymns for young people' and published by the Children's Special Services Mission), I cannot think of anything less suitable for children, for its contents reveal, even to the most fleeting of glances, a poverty of invention which explains why such a collection is today held up to ridicule. The real difference between the nineteenth and twentieth centuries lies in the extent of the influence of the hymn explosion of today and the consequent seeds for good which have been sown as a result.

Because of this, and arising from this, all and sundry have come up with aids, advice and guides concerning the choice of hymns. Virtually every new hymn book contains suggested lists for every conceivable occasion, while independent books further widen the range of possibilities by additionally taking in the themes for the Sundays as set out in the new lectionaries.

This profusion of guidelines has attendant dangers in that the chances are that we shall now never be required to think again for ourselves; we shall merely turn to ready made resource material. With everything consequently done for us, our powers of imagination need never more be tested or stretched. So we have turned full circle from the one extreme, where no help was available, to another, which on balance could be far more stultifying.

One of the commonest shortcomings is our failure to think about the words and to project their full meaning. Time and again in the singing of hymns it is the tune which provides the memorability, and with it the association. This well and truly puts the cart before the horse, the more so when we sally forth parrot fashion on a familiar hymn. How easily and all too readily our minds wander, we look around the church and in many instances, if we are honest, we get to the end oblivious of having given any heed to the words.

This of course can equally apply to anything which is familiar and repetitive, such as the saying of the Lord's Prayer, the Creed and the Grace. While such failings may be part and parcel of human nature, they quickly lead to a lack of regard for punctuation and the ignoring of crucial word stresses. If, as can all too easily happen, we sing 'How sweet the name of Jesus sounds' with every word and syllable given equal emphasis, together with the almost automatic compulsion to take a breath at the end of each line, our lack of awareness for the meaning of the words is all too obvious. By the reverse process, when we approach the words with real thought and insight, it results in a very different and far more convincing end product:

How sweet the name of Jes-us sounds

In a be-liev-er's ear;

In not unrelated terms I shall explore the clergy point of view equally with that of the musicians, although in an ideal situation the choice and use of hymns is a matter of joint concern and a joint responsibility, something which should apply to all aspects of the work of clergy and musicians.

While it needs to be recognized that, the world over, there are strong minded clergy bent on promoting music which many feel to be trivial and unworthy in theological and musical content, the purpose of this book is to deal mainly with the mainstream of what we might conveniently term either the 'establishment' or the traditional. Most fringe music, although it has a decidedly popular appeal in many churches, is as inherently ephemeral as it is instant and disposable. 'Pop' and allied music frequently has a short life which is the rational outcome of its nature and its make-up. We should accept it as such and not seek to invest it with a permanency it neither merits nor justifies.

My desire is to promote what I believe to be more lasting and which, through its staying power, has been abundantly proven to have more permanency. There is much fine hymnody of all periods, not least the contemporary, and it is these areas which will claim my attention in what follows.

Some practicalities

In most instances I will, for convenience of reference, quote from the New Standard Edition (NSE) of *Hymns Ancient and Modern* which was published in 1983. In addition to the 333 hymns which form its core and which were taken from *Hymns Ancient and Modern Revised* (1950), the two supplements *100 Hymns for Today* and *More Hymns for Today*, follow on as numbers 334 to 533.

There is a short bibliography on page 96, but I have also additionally drawn attention to some of these publications as and when they are relevant to any particular juncture in the main text. I have also presumed to include mention of my book *Church Music in a Changing World*, which was published by Mowbray in 1984. In it are restated certain hobby horses from other books and articles, but, in company with the preacher and the parent, I believe that there are certain things which need to be reiterated again and again.

Finally, my grateful thanks to those whose advice and superior knowledge I have sought in putting together this book. My especial gratitude is due to Canon Cyril Taylor and John Wilson, who have so generously dealt with my many queries and whose expertise on the subject of hymns and hymnody in general leaves us lesser mortals trailing along as best we can.

2
GENERAL POINTS OF DEPARTURE

What exactly is a hymn?

What constitutes a hymn, and when is a hymn not a hymn?

The original definition of a hymn is simply a song of praise, no more and no less. 'Hymn' is a Greek word and one that was in use long before the advent of the Christian era. In the first chapter of Erik Routley's *Christian Hymns Observed* the nature of hymnody is neatly outlined and summed up for us, in that basically they are 'songs for unmusical people to sing *together*', the final word (my italics) being the operative one. A hymn is further defined as 'a 'strophic song on a Christian subject capable of being sung by a congregation which was not in any sense made up of trained singers'.

It would be unthinkable to contemplate worship without encountering at one time or another some of the many hymns which are part and parcel of church-going the world over. Some, without denominational restriction, have assumed the significance and influence of becoming virtually ecclesiastical folk music, two such examples being 'Amazing grace' and 'Morning has broken'. These not only got themselves into the hymn charts some years ago but have remained there to this day and, moreover, show no signs of being displaced or dislodged.

Within the more traditional framework, 'Abide with me' and 'Guide me, O thou great Redeemer' to *Cwm Rhondda* may have had a much longer usage but have no less magnetism for churchgoers. In terms of the past thirty years *Blaenwern* and Cyril Taylor's tune *Abbot's Leigh* have by popular demand qualified to join these ranks. Such is their comprehensive use within the Church.

These are but a mere handful of examples which not only demonstrate how hymnody embraces and straddles the ecumenical scene but serves equally well to illustrate just how much hymns are written into the worship, witness and life of the Church. The fact that they exert such a significance and influence, which is not always immediately realized or thought through, is one of the main reasons for this book, in which I shall try to open windows and show insights as to what hymnody can achieve—and does achieve—in enriching worship when employed aright. Hymns, in a word, are basic and inescapable common denominators to the majority of worship situations.

The general and most widely understood definition of a hymn in terms of twentieth century thinking is to liken it to a poem, which in essence it is. This means that the lines not only rhyme but that they scan in a certain prescribed way—metre, as it is called in hymn terminology. A glance at the metrical index of tunes in any hymn book will show how certain metres are much more widely used than others, their special suitability having by long use and association made them immediately attractive and singable. CM (Common Metre) and LM (Long Metre) come very much within this category.

When is a hymn not a hymn? Parry's *Repton* is an example of music originally composed as a contralto aria—'Long since in Egypt's plenteous land'—in his oratorio *Judith.* Although it has gained a place in a number of hymn books ever since it first appeared in the Repton School Hymnal, the feel and mood, being that of a free composed song, places it in a different and certainly more problematic category than most other hymns. Even so, its splendid melodic line is its qualification.

Some hymns come into the quaintly named metrical category of 'irregular'. Holst's *Cranham*, set to Christina Rossetti's 'In the bleak mid-winter' (*AMR* 67) employs additional words and syllables to such an extent as to make accurate singing of this beautiful poem something of a rarity. It can certainly be something of a nightmare for many a choir, but more so for congregations. 'Thou didst leave thy throne and thy kingly crown' (*EH* 585) is a further instance not without its attendant problems, while 'For all the saints' to Vaughan Williams' *Sine nomine* (*EH* 641) is made the more difficult because no one really knows for certain how the composer intended the music to marry up to the words. The underlay of text and music at the beginning and at the end of some of the lines is seldom consistent and even less often correctly sung.

Some of the hymns of the 20th Century Church Light Music Group come into something of a hinterland in this respect. Although most of this collection is textually cast in metrical form, the interludes between the verses in some examples give a through composed end product, while the liberal use of an element of rubato which is sometimes included for good measure, can provide added difficulties. Hymns such as 'All glory, laud, and honour' (*AMR* 597) and 'Lift high the Cross' (*AMR* 633), although continuous in that there are no gaps between verses, are nevertheless cast in a familiar metrical mould.

A hymn is not a hymn as we generally understand it when it is what we so nebulously refer to as a chorus. Although this is not always easy to define in terms of church use, a study of *Sounds of Living Waters* and similar collections shows numerous examples where there is not always all that subtle a difference between a hymn and a chorus. Because the latter are linked more with evangelical and charismatic worship than with other types of service patterns, the distinction is perhaps easier to identify. Choruses, by their very nature, and certainly in their musical content, frequently benefit from an accompaniment other than the organ and for this reason are also the easier to distinguish.

Also, a hymn is not a hymn when it is what we loosely define in this context as a song. The identification is usually made the easier in that a song is generally for solo voice, as distinct from group performance by choir and congregation, the former probably singing in four part (SATB) harmony. The songs of Sydney Carter, in company with other 'protest' songs, are an example of what comes very much within this category.

A reliable guideline for identifying a hymn in the accepted sense is the look of it on the printed page with the tune above the words which are set out like a poem. The one exception to this is to be found in most hymn books in the United States, where the text will usually be printed between the two staves of the music. While this has the visual advantage, or convenience, of having words and music printed above and below each other, it precludes reading the text as poetry, a major disadvantage which the ubiquitous Erik Routley was quick to seize on and which he was adamant in denouncing as detracting from the American understanding of the poetic nature of hymns.

In all hymnody, as in all song, it is essential that we recognize the words as the first consideration and that, as in all vocal music, the words are enriched, are carried a stage further and given an added impetus or bonus, call it what you will, through their being clothed with music. This is the *raison d'etre* of all song, be it folk music, the operas of Mozart, the songs of Schubert and Brahms, or Gilbert and Sullivan.

In terms of hymnody it therefore follows that words and music should ideally fit each other like a glove.

Despite this requisite, which is basic to all vocal music, it is regrettable, as mentioned in Chapter 1, that the popular association of hymnody lies for many of us in an almost total preoccupation with the music and not with the words. But it is the music which characterizes the memorability of most hymns. This is perhaps to an extent understandable if we pause to consider how much is lacking in the poetry, theology and teaching of some of the hymns so dear to the hearts of church-goers. This is a classic example of blind acceptance without stopping to think.

Why do we use hymns?

Leaving aside their long historical association with the Church and their resulting significance as integral parts of Christian worship, it is undeniable that song is instinctive to most of us, whether we be in church or not. The employment of hymnody as being crucial to public worship is as old as the Christian Church itself, even older if we take note of Old Testament allusions to its use. We often fail to recognize the inevitability of music in any worship situation, the more so when we narrow this down to hymns because, of all musical pursuits within the Church, the singing of hymns is, or should be, inclusive in its involvement of all concerned.

Hymns underline in a particular way the multiplicity of events within the calendar of the Church's year. They equally reinforce other specific occasions such as baptisms, weddings and funerals. In a wider context they mark certain focal points within a liturgical service, such as the Introit, the Gradual, the Offertory, and before or after the sermon. They can also serve to highlight processions, but only if approached in a correct liturgical sense. It is an abuse of the function of a procession merely to walk in to a service or recess out at the end of it singing a hymn, a procedure which totally ignores the historical reason or purpose for a procession (see page 89).

The various uses of hymnody, their significance, and, more importantly, what they can achieve when chosen and used correctly, will be matters for discussion in the following pages. Their power to emphasize, underline, and carry a stage further what is said in readings, sermons and teaching generally, is as applicable to the Anglican Church as it is fundamental to Free Church worship. The denominator common to *all* hymns is that of music conceived for and intended to be sung by the entire worshipping body, as distinct from those occasions when the choir alone will perhaps be responsible for musical extras.

The case for the involvement of all in the singing of hymns is not only an historical one but is also determined by a general consensus of opinion as to the purpose underlying hymnody.

As the misuses, even sometimes the abuses, are constantly in evidence, this will be a further matter for discussion and something I shall try to help resolve. Hymns are not merely pleasant interludes nor should they be employed to cover up what might otherwise be awkward silences. Chosen, positioned, and used with care, they provide unique insights into a particularly essential aspect of worship. Over the years, and especially during this century, hymns have become more and more integral to worship as a commonly shared element within every denomination. We see this from the Bach chorale, through Luther, Isaac Watts and Newman, to the 'gospel' hymns of the nineteenth century revival, the twentieth century chorus and, not least, to the emergence of a significant group of hymn writers in our time.

All this, and more, is contained within a vast corpus of material. In a word, the world is our oyster, resulting in so many rich treasures available for our use, our edification and our enjoyment.

The extent to which the Church has always heavily relied on the use of hymns cannot be overestimated. It should therefore shame us that all too easily we can approach the subject quite casually or, conversely, readily encourage congregations in what they believe to be their almost mandatory right to have a good 'sing' at every conceivable opportunity, whether it be liturgically correct or not. This is especially relevant to the end of ASB Rite A Holy Communion and is one of the many pertinent observations made by Alan Dunstan in *Interpreting Worship* (Mowbray). This admirable little book should, incidentally, be mandatory reading matter for all church musicians.

There are those responsible for choosing hymns who do so with a modicum of care or concern, while the musicians, likewise, in their turn are sometimes guilty of performing them with an absence of responsibility. Musicians who give priority to anthems while relegating hymns as unavoidable intrusions have, as I mentioned at the outset and reiterate here, confused—and abused—their priorities. These attitudes strike at the heart of the matter, as so many know from what they experience Sunday by Sunday.

We do well to note the Free Churches who, because they place so much emphasis on hymns, even though this may be in default of the use of relatively little other music, can nevertheless teach us Anglicans a great deal in this connection.

'He that hath ears . . .'

3
KNOWING WHAT IS AVAILABLE

Before 1950, it was all a fairly predicable scene, especially if you were C. of E. It was also, by comparison with the growth and range of material which is available today, a somewhat sparse arena.

Hymns Ancient and Modern, then as now, was to the forefront as probably the most widely used Anglican collection. Prior to the 1950 edition it was a drab looking affair both within and without. Its unattractive dark blue cover could hardly be calculated to 'sell' it, as would an attractive gramophone record sleeve. But sell it did, and in vast numbers, and this despite the typography and general layout, which was ecclesiastical Gothic of the worst kind and which could hardly have inspired confidence or enthusiasm to delve deeper into what lay inside. The book of course contained much of value, the best of which, together with a considerable amount of new material, found its way into *Hymns Ancient and Modern Revised* (1950). This, by marked contrast, is in every way a much more attractive and engaging proposition to look at, to handle and, not least, to use.

A and M's nearest rival was *The English Hymnal*, especially if you had leanings towards a 'high church' expression and wanted to use plainchant, office hymns and other material for saints' days. If you had a penchant for the folk song revival, so much the better; with Vaughan Williams as its musical editor this was hardly surprising.

Songs of Praise also catered for similar eclectic needs

though, on balance, and seen now in retrospect, it is a slightly recherché collection with a section of hymns for children exemplifying some of the worst excesses to be found anywhere, however much it may have been slanted towards what in the 1920s and 1930s were considered to be the spiritual needs of young people.

In a somewhat different category was *The Public School Hymn Book*, a fine collection, much of which, both in words and music, was admirable for schools and their needs at that time. This was revised and updated in 1964 when it became *Hymns for Church and School*, a thoroughly admirable book in every way.

On the fringe should be mentioned *The Oxford Hymn Book* (1908) and *The Yattendon Hymnal* (1899), both beautifully and distinctively produced. The latter was the brain child of the poet Robert Bridges, and was compiled for the village church of that name near Newbury in Berkshire. It is a fascinating anthology, beautifully designed and a book collector's delight, as is *Chants for the Psalter—Yattendon*. Whether the former is a viable collection in terms of today's needs is another matter.

A number of books fitfully lingered on during the war and even into the 1960s. One of the most depressing of these was *The Church and School Hymnal* where, at number 277, we find words which it is inconceivable to think of as being used today. Yet this particular hymn does, or did, live on and I for one sometimes heard it during my Exeter days being lustily, if not entirely convincingly, sung in one or two of the Devon village churches—and sung by adults as well as by children:

O once in a while
  We obey with a smile
And are ever so modest and prudent,
  But it's not very long
Before something is wrong
  And somebody's done what he shouldn't.

In meadow and wood
  The cattle are good
And the rabbits are thinking no evil;
  The anemones white
Are refined and polite
  And all the primroses are civil.

O Saviour, look down
  When we sulk or we frown
And smooth into kindness our quarrels;
  Till our heart is as light
As a little bird's flight
  And our life is as free as a squirrel's!

Other hymn books, while not perhaps reflecting quite the same sentiments, certainly showed a predictability which was distinctly greyish. Most collections were produced in the same type of dull format as the Standard Edition of *A and M* and much of their content was equally uneventful. There is so much we just would not—or should not—use today, simply because most of us now think differently about texts, the theology of which in some instances is, if we are honest, extremely dubious and suspect.

Meanwhile, far better and more suitable tunes have overtaken some which had previously reigned supreme and unchallenged.

Every so often society—and the Church is no exception—throws up a revolution which dramatically changes the face and direction of what it supersedes. Such was 'The Hymn Explosion', and how aptly termed was that exciting and immensely fruitful period between around 1955 and 1980. It revolutionized the entire scene and opened up enormous vistas never previously conceived or envisaged; it also formulated the best of what we today rejoice in.

This, together with the liturgical revolution, which in terms of worship patterns began at the same time to sweep across the entire spectrum of Christendom, has changed the church going habits and thinking of very many people. New hymn books, and supplements to old ones, have mushroomed across the length and breadth of the Christian Church. Parallel to this, and importantly complementary to it, has been the spate of books on the subject of hymnody, many of them perceptively scholarly and helpfully critical. To the forefront in all this was Erik Routley, with others such as Alan Dunstan, John Wilson and Cyril Taylor contributing their wide and unique range of scholarship and knowledge.

The words and music of many hymns have been recast over the centuries, while others which had lain in limbo, or had been forgotten, have now been rediscovered. Much of this has been triggered off by the cumulative thrust of contemporary interest and the scholarship mentioned just now. Here in Britain, as in the United States, there is a significant Hymn Society, while almost every year there is in Europe or in the United States a conference of hymnologists dealing with a remarkably wide range of highly detailed subject matter. Hymnody is now being studied assiduously with invaluable results being fed back for all to benefit from.

So much for what we might term the 'traditional' aspect. When the 20th Century Church Light Music Group came on to the scene in the 1960s, it heralded the start of a move which, by marked contrast with the general thrust of traditional hymnody, has tentacled out into a multiplicity of endeavour, with choruses—charismatic or otherwise—'pop' music, folk songs and, not least, music for children, presenting a wide spread of new invention.

Musically and textually, much of this is questionable, if only for the endlessly repetitive and jingoistic musical phrases which are frequently partnered by a similar repetitiveness of words. It is one thing to suggest certain words and statements to emphasize a central theme, as did Patrick Appleford in 'Jesus, humble was your birth', but an entirely different matter to produce a 'hymn' which says:

> Jesus, Jesus, Jesus, Jesus,
> Jesus, Jesus, Jesus, Jesus,
> Jesus, Jesus, Jesus, Jesus,
> Jesus, Jesus, Jesus, Jesus.

underneath which, I am told, was proudly printed 'Words copyright'.

It is also one thing to sing the tune *St Denio* where three of the four musical lines are the same, but a rather different proposition to mechanically repeat a group of notes *ad nauseam*. In the end, what is there to choose between the two?

As I pointed out in Chapter 2, there is more than a subtle distinction between a chorus and a hymn. While I accept that there is a role as much for the chorus as for the traditional hymn, there is nevertheless a sharp distinction between the music and the texts of the one as compared with the other. But perhaps we are wrong to compare and should leave each to pursue its separate way, providing the more popular is not foisted on to a congregation more reluctant than willing to accept what they find embarrassing. However well intentioned the eager young curate or the mature vicar may be in this respect, gentle persuasion will often achieve more than the press-gang method.

My final point on this subject concerns the expendability of some of the more novel trends. As with the 'pop' song, its life may well be, and ought to be, a short-lived one. Some would argue, and not without a grain of truth, that certain examples of our more traditional hymnody should have been similarly treated.

One of the real problems besetting hymns is, as I mentioned in Chapter 1, that most people think of the music first, and it is therefore the music, not the words, that influences the majority of people.

A further problem confronting hymns is that for most people the music is what determines a good hymn, with the words, if they even stop to think about them, coming very much as a secondary consideration. While this is obviously putting the cart before the horse, it is something which, because of its long habit, is difficult to dislodge.

The greatest advance in our time has been not so much the music as the wealth of poets who have emerged and whose sum total of effort has, almost without exception, provided an entirely new concept. To take only three examples, even if they are outstandingly obvious ones, there is Bishop Stewart Cross, who wrote 'Father, Lord of all Creation' (*NSE* 356), Brian Wren's 'I come with joy to meet my Lord' (*NSE* 473)—and what a splendid 'going out into the world' hymn this is—and Erik Routley's 'New songs of celebration render' (*NSE* 498). Nor must the rediscovery of a number of hymns by writers of previous generations go unheeded; for example, Isaac Watts' 'Lord, I have made thy word my choice' (*NSE* 490) and 'Give to our God immortal praise'(*NSE* 460). Both are superb examples of Watts, the former a paraphrase of part of Psalm 119. But these are only two from among many fine hymns which have found new life and usage through our new hymn books.

One of the most prolific of contemporary hymn writers is Fred Pratt Green, a Methodist minister whose work can be found in profusion and without exception in all the self-respecting collections of recent years. Slightly less in output but no less significant in this interdenominational line-up is the work of Brian Wren, Timothy Dudley-Smith, Brian Foley and John Bowers. The latter appears no less than seven times in *More Hymns for Today*.

Hymnody today is a serious preoccupation, even if

the average person in the pew takes it for granted and ceases to show much further interest at that point, unless of course a favourite hymn which happens to be an old friend is ousted.

Further prominence has been given through radio and television, with weekly programmes such as the BBC's *Songs of Praise* and *Sunday Half Hour* drawing extremely large audiences. ITV provides an even wider range, though much of it is variable in content and certainly in a generally more popular mould.

The vogue for hymns and hymn singing finds a further outlet in the many gramophone records coming from every conceivable source. From time to time competitions are mounted, either for new words or for new music, although the outcome is not always necessarily what some would consider to be the best choice. Notwithstanding the inevitable hazards of competitions and the particular viewpoints of adjudicators, this is a healthy sign of interest, activity and encouragement. Whether the end product of all the media activity in this respect is, in the long run, a good thing is another matter; it is also debatable whether, on balance, however much the immediate interest is encouraging, lasting good results.

The overall scene today

The sum total of what is currently available reveals in no uncertain way how lucky we are, yet the almost dazzling array can make a decision on what book or supplement to adopt a daunting affair. It is essential to know what each collection seeks to promote—and they all promote different lines and policies—and then to relate this to the overall needs of the church in question. This demands not only studying a number of books and seeking advice from experts, but doing so with all viewpoints represented in committee—the clergy, the musicians and, perhaps most important of all, the congregation. What should always be resisted is for the incumbent to dictate and to foist his personal preference on to his flock. The final decision should be a consensus of opinion which, in its turn, has allowed a necessary element of give and take.

In what follows, I have tried to highlight certain particular features and policy which underlines the direction a number of books have taken.

Hymns Ancient and Modern

The 1950 edition offloaded from the blue Standard Edition those hymns which had never really found favour, together with others that the editors 'felt could well be spared, yet undoubtedly they were endeared to quite a number of congregations.' Some tunes, however, which by 1950 had become popular in various fields were not available for the new edition because of copyright restrictions, the most notable being Vaughan Williams' *Down Ampney* and *Sine Nomine.*

The 1950 edition brought in some fine old tunes, notably French Church melodies of the seventeenth and eighteenth centuries. The Preface, as informative as in previous editions, proudly proclaimed, 'The new book does not aim at breaking fresh ground or exploiting novel ideas.'

100 Hymns for Today appeared in 1969 with the introduction claiming that, 'Today's Christians need today's songs to sing as well as yesterday's. The great hymns of the past need no patronage or recommendation. But we cannot live only on the achievements of the past.' This innovatory collection contained *all* new material, none of which was in any of the past editions of A and M. It also led the way to being the first of countless supplements and new books to come from virtually every denomination.

Some less traditional hymns, such as those of Beaumont and Appleford, also found their niche, though in general terms the 'contemporary' examples are good without resorting to the pursuit of gimmicky or ephemeral idioms.

In a word, the aim was a middle course, which was novel in two respects. While many of the modern hymn writers do not use the rhymes and metres of an older age, this book also took a new line as compared with those of the last century which assumed 'a society more agricultural than industrial, untroubled by questions of race relations and human rights'. But it also presupposed a Church influenced by the fierce conflicts of this century. 'A good Christian hymn will always say something, coherent, and will not merely express passing feelings and momentary attitudes.' So spake the Preface once again.

100 Hymns for Today had an overwhelming success and was followed in 1981 by *More Hymns for Today.* The intervening twelve years revealed an unexpected and thoroughly exciting outburst of hymns, not only in England but throughout the world. This second supplement continued to cater, but in an expanded way, for Holy Communion, Baptism, Weddings and Harvest. Isaac Watts, Charles Wesley and other predictables are there side by side with an impressive array of twentieth century hymn poets.

More Hymns for Today was not intended as a substitute for either *100 Hymns for Today* or *Ancient and Modern Revised,* but to be used as supplementary material alongside these other books.

As with *100 Hymns for Today,* it 'seeks to be forward looking without abandoning ordered restraint; to be sensitive to the changing needs and renewed vitality of the Church in a turbulent world, while being rooted in the long, living tradition of the people of God.' Both supplements, incidentally, contain much needed short 'connecting' hymns or for going out at the end of a service.

Four or five years ago it was decided that the main 1950 edition *(Hymns Ancient and Modern Revised)*, needed a reappraisal. It had, after all, been in existence for three decades, and ones of great change at that. It contained many hymns little used today, or not used at all. These are therefore omitted from the New Standard Edition which was first published in June 1983. A few revisions in words and music are made but, so far as is possible, the new book is deliberately designed to be used side by side with the 1950 edition, thus contributing towards a continuing, and necessary, process of both offloading and taking on board. This has resulted in 333 of the 636 hymns in the Revised Edition being retained together with the two supplements.

There are two major innovations. The generally lower keys, referred to elsewhere in this book, although welcomed by congregations were less enthusiastically received by choirs, and understandably so. White notation has in general been dispensed with in favour of crotchets and quavers, these being easier to read.

No modernizing of 'thee' and 'thou' language was embarked upon, nor was anything 'sexist' altered to satisfy the 'voices of feminine emancipation'. It was thought right not to change the words of hymns to meet this objection. 'We believe that in this new form a book which has long been highly valued in the life and worship of Christians will continue to strengthen the life of the Church.'

The English Hymnal was first published in 1906, with Vaughan Williams as its musical editor. Among the individual features which make it distinct from *Hymns Ancient and Modern* is the inclusion of no less than eighty hymns for saints days and other holy days. All the categories of saints, including confessors, virgins, matrons, together with the vigils, are provided for, but of course only taking into account those which were currently observed prior to the advent of the ASB.

A sizeable section deals with 'special occasions' which range from 'absent friends' to 'temperance societies' and 'time of rough weather'. Other distinctive features of this all embracing collection are the thirty-four hymns for use in procession, together with litanies for a variety of occasions, introits, the Advent antiphons, the Advent and Lent proses and the Reproaches, all in plainchant.

English Praise, the 1975 supplement to the main book, picks up a wide range of new material for most occasions, almost all of which was not in the parent book. There are also eight admirable responsorial psalms, the work of Dom Gregory Murray.

The New English Hymnal, which will contain 500 examples, is due sometime in 1985. Apart from a revised music edition in 1933, this will be the first major overhaul since 1906. Innovations include a further group of liturgical hymns, a large section for the Eucharist together with Proper hymns, including a number of new ones for all the red letter saints days in the 1980 calendar.

In the liturgical section, twenty-seven texts are included which now embrace sequences for a number of occasions which were not previously catered for, such as Pentecost, Corpus Christi and All Souls.

All in all, this should help in providing for the needs of those churches for whom the *English Hymnal* has always offered the right mix.

The Anglican Hymn Book is basically a collection for Evangelicals. On its publication in 1965 it came in for considerable criticism for it was one of the innovators in altering the texts of some of the more familiar hymns. On the other hand, it was equally called to account for omitting some of the favourites, such as

'Lead, kindly light' and 'Nearer, my God, to Thee', while failing to include a lot of new material which was available. Nevertheless, this book appeared at a time when the full impact of modern hymn writing had only just begun to be realized, and it should be given credit for including a modicum of innovation, even if some of this was more musically extended than we would today consider right, or perhaps feasible, in terms of congregational participation.

With One Voice was initially published as *The Australian Hymn Book*. It was the work of five different denominations, which undoubtedly accounts for much of its enviable inclusiveness. Two years later, in 1979, it was published in Britain by Collins as *With One Voice*, but minus the Catholic supplement of forty-four hymns which were in the original Australian book.

There is certainly much in this book to commend it. With nearly a quarter of its contents from the twentieth century, it can claim to be forward looking, and this it is without being in any way trendy. Erik Routley, who knew more about hymnody than most people, hailed it as 'just about the most encouraging thing I have seen in the past generation.' It is without doubt a collection to be seriously considered, as much for what it contains as for the way in which it is designed and printed. As such, it is a far cry from the Standard Edition of *Hymns Ancient and Modern* mentioned earlier.

Songs of the People of God, published as its companion, is precisely what it sets out to be and is good value in every way. It not only gives notes on each hymn, its tune, and the personalities involved, but also includes three aptly named sections on 'the obligations' of clergy, organists and choirmasters.

Hymns for Church and School is the fourth edition of *The Public School Hymn Book*. Although obviously designed primarily for school use, this fine collection should not on that account be ruled out of court for a wider usage. Musically, it is significant and to be highly rated. While there are no concessions to the more popular style of tune such as The 20th Century Church Light Music Group, it is well worth a careful study, which will reveal some surprising treasures and an unexpected degree of suitability to many parish situations. To take but one random example, look at the exciting, and authentic, version of Handel's well known tune *Gopsal.*

Hymns for Today's Church. Long before this book appeared in 1982, there was a calculated and widespread publicity build-up on its claims to being *the* present day answer to the language we should be using in hymnody. It argued that because the language of worship has moved into a new and contemporary era, it is anachronistic to sing hymns employing dated language, thoughts and, not least, images. In the event, the anticipation was on publication tempered, even perhaps reversed, by equally widespread adverse criticism, much of which, especially in the national press, was strongly condemnatory.

Further fuel for the fire was the fact that up to a quarter of the new material in the book came from the editors or was by their friends, who were very much on an identical wavelength of thought and commitment.

While we are all only too aware of the arguments for and against employing contemporary language, there is the viewpoint, which I happen to share, that whereas you can update with impunity the language of the Book of Common Prayer, the psalms of Coverdale and the King James Bible, it is an entirely different and much more problematic matter to contemplate tinkering with the words of hymns. Many of these are time honoured and known in their original form by all concerned and, more importantly, they are in many instances inseparably linked with well established music, and vice versa.

These then are but some of the Anglican books. There are of course many more, some in print, some long out of print, with others such as *Songs of Praise* only minimally used nowadays. Into a similar category comes the *BBC Hymn Book* together with its supplement *Broadcast Praise*, both of which were devised initially for use with the daily service broadcasts.

For the future, hymn enthusiasts eagerly await the long heralded and meticulously prepared new American Episcopal Hymnal announced for late 1985. Its title, *The Hymnal 1982*, may seem somewhat strange, but the committee responsible worked to a strictly defined system and drew the line at excluding any new material which appeared after 1982. Even so, it will have taken all of three years to get the final choice into shape and then into print.

On the 'fringe', in a definitive rather than a derogatory sense, come collections such as *Youth Praise* and *Psalm Praise*. Here are hymns and especially choruses for a need entirely different from what we have so far been considering, namely for young people meeting and worshipping in an informal way. Both met—and I reservedly say this in the past tense because I believe this to be relevant to the 1960s and 1970s, which saw their inception—a need which was then being felt for a distinctively twentieth century melodic idiom. Many of the hymns in these collections were therefore for unison singing as opposed to SATB while much was peripheral, such as the protest songs which rejoiced in telling God what he ought to be doing.

Much of the failure of their staying power probably lies in the music rather than in the words. It is, as Robin Leaver observed, 'all very much in the same rather superficial style. It is a weakness shared with other similar books where most of the music comes from a smallish group of composers who share the same ideals and concepts.' (Robin Leaver: *A Hymn Book Survey 1962–80*, Grove Worship Series No. 71, page 17.)

Into a somewhat similar category comes *Sound of Living Waters* and its companion volume *Fresh Sounds*, published by Hodder and Stoughton in 1974 and 1976. The titles reflect the objectives of the compilers, for here indeed are some fresh sounds, albeit linked with the Charismatic Movement. Even so, much of what these books contain is anything but new, a fact which many did not at first perceive. To hear, as I recently did in South Africa, 'I heard the voice of Jesus say' sung unaccompanied but for a delightful flute obbligato, to the beautiful folk tune *Kingsfold*, is an experience I shall long remember, as much for the beauty of its sound as for its aptness in a Sunday evening Communion Service at a church in Port Elizabeth.

Partners in Praise (1979) is but one of the collections to have come from Galliard, those stalwart champions publishing hymnody with a distinctive hallmark which would never claim to be remotely related to books such as *Hymns Ancient and Modern*. Unlike its predecessors, and to quote Robin Leaver again, 'It tackles the difficult problem "How do we prepare so that the event is not an occasion for adults with children looking on, or for children with adults on the sidelines?" ' (ibid. p. 19).

On the non-Anglican front are new books and new supplements issuing with great profusion from the various denominations. There are far too many to mention here without the risk of omitting some at the expense of others. Such is the ever present—though highly challenging and encouraging—dilemma of trying to keep up with all that is being produced.

No hymn book, radical or otherwise, and whatever its denominational birthright, will ever be perfect for all concerned nor meet all demands in their entirety. Such a Utopia is incapable of attainment. Tastes, preferences, even bigoted views, let alone churchmanship, whether we opt for traditional fare, whether it be choruses or whether we have trendy inclinations, are all valid considerations which conspire to make this a most difficult and problematic pursuit.

If asked to single out one recent other than Anglican book, I would opt for *Hymns and Psalms*, the new Methodist book. Why?

It is always a salutory and thoroughly informative exercise to read the preface or introduction to any hymn book. Because this is something most of us seldom do, I unreservedly commend it, for it does at least reveal what the compilers were trying to do, and no two books have identical policies or aims as the same end product or objective. Such is true of *Hymns and Psalms*, the successor to The Methodist Hymn Book of 1933. Devised by an ecumenical group, this in itself was a fairly radical departure. The end product shows a third of its contents as being new to Methodism or to ecumenism. Fair enough, for its sub-title is 'A Methodist and Ecumenical Hymn Book'.

What materialized was a truly contemporary hymn book in that it 'articulates the needs, the joys, and the fears of the contemporary world', which are reflected in its three distinct sections. These deal with God's Nature, God's World and God's People. Gone are the page headings which were a feature of many of the Victorian hymn books. There was even, I am told, one nineteenth century book which made provision for 'backsliders recovered' and 'mourners convinced of sin'. None of that in the new Methodist book; even 'general hymns', that ubiquitous and vague heading found in so many books, has also disappeared.

As congregational singing was an almost over-riding concern, the book was not designed exclusively for occasions when choirs are an essential feature. All the usual indexes one would expect to find are there, with the Sunday themes and useful guidelines based on biblical texts.

Thirty-nine hymns of Isaac Watts and no less than one hundred and fifty-six of Charles Wesley account for nearly one-quarter of the contents; but this is probably no bad thing, for the latter did at least preach doctrine as compared with the ethics which are so prevalent today.

In practical terms, one regrets no melody-only edition, the more so as the 823 hymns alone, quite apart from the other material such as psalms, make it a decidedly bulky and heavy book.

Summarizing

Taken as a whole, the great hymns of all time will always be in vogue and will find a place in most, if not all, orthodox collections. There is so much which is common ground to all denominations.

The problem is in deciding how, and what, to take from one book or from another. Is it in fact wise to do just this? Maybe there is something to be said for a do-it-yourself loose-leaf collection to which you add or discard as you wish, though in this there is always the problem of copyright.

In the end, the world is your oyster, and it would be imprudent to suggest, other than through generalized guidelines, how one might proceed. The hymn arena is a constantly widening and expanding one which provides a challenge, even if in practice it can sometimes be frustrating. One can only write of the situation as it pertains at this moment in time.

When a church is contemplating changing over to a new book, how one makes what one believes to be the right choice will always be a debatable matter needing much care and thought.

My final comment on this subject may be something of an apology, for I fully realize that I have omitted mention of a number of candidates, and that champions will rise up, probably in great wrath, proclaiming the virtues of those books I have not mentioned as against those I have elected to write about. How good it is that there are people whose allegiance dictates opinionated viewpoints. This surely is how it should be.

4

GENERAL HINTS ON CHOICE

Whose task is it?

In many instances this is done by the clergy, and with good reason. As overall authority for the ordering of services is vested with the clergy, it is only right that the important matter of hymns should come within their brief. Also, quite apart from the special needs of festivals and other occasions, the preacher may want to use a specific hymn as an additional teaching focus to preface or follow the sermon.

On the other hand, left as it is in some instances to the organist, the choice of hymns can be less than relevant, if only for the fact that some organists tend to put musical considerations first. I quite frankly doubt the wisdom of letting the organist loose on this important matter or even to expect him to make the choice on his own. It places an unreasonable burden on the shoulders of someone who is usually less than fully qualified in this respect. This is the more pertinent when, as can sometimes happen, the clergy are too lazy to be bothered to choose the hymns.

I would suggest it is a far better policy—and compromise—if clergy and organist jointly choose the hymns, and that whenever parson and organist meet to do so, the parson comes armed with his suggested outline choice. This provides a useful and sensible point of departure, though the parson should have the final say. This is his right, and his ultimate responsibility.

In this way the best of both worlds can result with, incidentally but highly desirable, the one probably progressing a stage further in finding out what makes the other tick. This can additionally help to cement the partnership which should be foremost in the sights of clergy and organist alike.

Arriving at the right choice is the concern of both parties, hymns being so important an element in any church service where there is to be music. The organist can, and should, suggest the choice of tunes and consequently help to avoid such situations as the indigestible placing of two hymns in the same key and metre, the one following the other. However apt the text of each hymn may be, this is wearisome to sing.

In the process of consultation with his clergy, the organist may also come to learn something of the theology of hymnody, which is no bad thing for any church musician.

If the parson is unmusical, he will as often as not resort to what is familiar to him; but this is by no means always a reliable, or wise, thermometer.

To take this a stage further, why not involve a member of the congregation who has an open mind and an interest in the subject and who might well have an additional and significant viewpoint to add, which will reflect something of the thinking of the congregation, those sometimes all but musically ignored people on the receiving end. More of this later.

General principles

In the Holy Communion Service of most denominations, the positioning of hymns is generally well defined by long established custom, though in the contemporary rites a greater measure of flexibility is allowed for. While this has its advantages, it can lead to certain difficulties unless a carefully agreed method of procedure has been worked out and agreed on by all parties concerned.

Suggestions as to how many hymns there should be

in any one service will be discussed on pages 41 and 47. At this stage I would merely emphasize certain factors, such as the need to think through some of what I would suggest are the disadvantages of cluttering up with hymns every available moment during the communion of the people. In a similar way the place for the final hymn in the Anglican Holy Communion Rite A or Rite B needs to be carefully thought through. There are now a number of admirable—and short—'going out into the world' hymns such as, from *A and M New Standard Edition:*

239. Forth in thy name, O Lord, I go
276. From glory to glory advancing
358. Father, who in Jesus found us
403. Now let us from this table rise
416. Praise the Lord, rise up rejoicing
436. Awake, our souls; away, our fears
458. Forth in the peace of Christ we go
510. Sent forth by God's blessing

These lose much of their effect if sung *after* the dismissal. The recommended places for these give carefully considered indications as to the best moment for the final hymn. Gone are, or should be, the days when we begin and end every service *de rigeur* with a hymn.

Similarly, in the Church of England's Morning and Evening Prayer (BCP or ASB), the suggested places for hymns are clearly defined and proven in practice. The function and place of the office hymn will be dealt with in Chapter 7.

The use and placing of hymns in special free structured services, not least in family services, needs to be equally carefully considered. Here are none of the constraints, however minimal, of liturgical services. The resultant impact of a hymn can therefore frequently be the more forceful in such situations. Because of this, not only must the choice obviously aim to be the most suitable, but other considerations need to be taken into account such as, in a family service, the possible mix of traditional hymns with the more 'popular' types, sometimes with the use of choruses and hymns for children.

How to satisfactorily integrate hymns for adults with those for children and vice versa, whether young and not so young should be expected to participate together, and whether there is a magical age when children move on to 'adult' hymns, are matters which need to be carefully thought through with the specific needs of each and every situation always in mind. Maybe a compromise is the answer, though this will not necessarily be the right solution in every case.

Then there is the question of some of the hymns which many of us sang as children a generation ago. Because many of these are less frequently encountered in schools nowadays, or are sometimes even unknown, it is wise, when looking for material for children to use in church, first to check with schools as to exactly what the children are accustomed to. Much of what is contained in the 'For Children' section of many standard hymn books is outmoded and frequently unknown to present day children. What has superseded this is often far more meaningful in words and much more attractive in musical content.

Because of this, children can understandably be put off by many of the more traditional hymns, which by their nature are much more four square. Children should, moreover, be encouraged to bring with them into church the instruments they use to accompany contemporary songs. They are probably far more suitable than the organ. This then leaves the way clear for the adults to sing their more traditional hymns with organ accompaniment. By doing this, all parties and interests should ideally be catered for and fulfilled, with no one particular faction feeling in any way threatened or even embarrassed by being expected to take part in something they sense not to be their scene.

It all reverts back to the dictum that, whatever the situation and whatever the service, hymns are integral to worship and, furthermore, actively involve all taking part in worship.

An overall general principle governing the choice of hymns should be that of variety. Ideally, a big hymn, such as 'Praise my soul, the King of heaven' needs to be followed by one that is small scale, 'Blest are the pure in heart' or 'Be thou my guardian and my guide' providing the sort of contrast needed.

Similarly, a basically loud hymn, of which there are so many, benefits from being placed next to a quieter one. The juxtaposition of hymns in major and minor keys is a further way of providing variation as will be the contrasted–and blessed–relief of having a short hymn of two or three verses only following five verses each of eight lines.

All these considerations obviously have to be matched with the suitability of each and every example to the needs of a specific juncture in a service. These in their turn are contributory factors in making the choice of hymns a demanding and time consuming occupation.

Further thoughts on the integration of the familiar with the new are outlined in Chapter 5.

The generally narrow choice in operation

With the bonanza of all that is now available, the world is our oyster. It is the more regrettable that the resulting choice is often so narrow, so repetitive, and consequently so unadventurous in using the many riches that are with us today as compared with a century ago. The plea that we must play safe and use 'the old familiar hymns' otherwise the congregation will revolt, may have some substance in certain situations. In others it can predictably react in the opposite direction.

There is no reason why a balanced diet of the familiar

with the less familiar and the new cannot be arrived at. The resultant situation will then be far healthier all round, if only because so much of the new is good, often superior to some of the old, certainly in language, theology, and in relevance to worship today.

I wonder how many churches keep a record of the hymns sung in any one year, together with an indication of the frequency of repetition. I suggest this could in many instances be revealing. Furthermore, I wonder how often members of the congregation are in fact involved or consulted over the choice of hymns which, incidentally, is so often male dominated. In this, as in so many matters, female input can present an entirely new and valuable viewpoint which we men would be wise to heed.

I also question in how many instances the congregation are invited to make their suggestions. Some of what would transpire may not, for one reason or another, be practicable but, nevertheless, it could be a most useful contribution.

Being in the congregation and therefore on the receiving end, as I now invariably find myself on Sundays, forcibly brings home to me the inadequacy of the choice of hymns in many instances. I also hazard a guess that those around me were probably never consulted or included in any deliberations on the subject.

While appreciating that in an ideal situation the end product will be the best choice as determined by consensus, one realizes that, however sophisticated the machinery may be for this purpose, we can never hope to please all shades of opinion. Nevertheless, all interests ranging from the children and teenagers through to senior citizens should surely be brought into consultation. Consideration must necessarily be given to situations which are other than traditional while taking into account the availability of resources needed to make this practicable.

Copyright

A word of warning here. The wide range of published hymnody in current circulation was discussed in Chapter 3. The temptation to extract a particular example from a collection, to reproduce it in any quantity, and hope to get away with it, is to a degree understandable, if only on the grounds of the expense factor involved in buying sets of a complete book. In most instances it is nevertheless illegal to do this without first seeking permission.

The Copyright Law can be something of a jungle to those unfamiliar with its ramifications. Although there are many situations within which it is perfectly in order to photocopy, there are equally many situations when it is not. Guide books exist, of which *Caution–Copyright!* by Eric A. Thorn (Third Day Enterprises/3D Music, PO Box 3, Maidstone, Kent ME14 1AP) is one of the best I know, in that it is particularly helpful. The golden rule is always to ask, never to take anything for granted, and certainly never to deliberately flaunt any restrictions. Those who say, 'I'll photocopy and be damned' deserve to be called to account. The law, moreover, does not allow nor accept ignorance as an excuse.

In the end, to ignore copyright restrictions is to play with fire, as a number of people have recently discovered.

Aids

With so many guides now available, together with the comprehensive subject indexes contained in many hymn books and, in more recent ones, linked with the Sunday themes in the new lectionary, there is no excuse for failing to come up with a menu of hymns which is both relevant and full of variety.

Three specific publications can be recommended as invaluable guides:

1. *The Year's Praise* (The St Andrew Press, 121 George Street, Edinburgh, EH2 4YN) 1976.
   This contains praise lists for two years of services following the order of the Christian year. For use with *The Church Hymnary*, Third Edition (1973).
2. *Hymns with the New Lectionary*, compiled by Robin Leaver (Grove Books, Bramcote, Notts) 1980.
   This covers over twenty books.
3. *A Hymn Guide for the Sunday Themes of the New Lectionary in the Alternative Service Book 1980* (Mowbray) 1981.
   Compiled by members of the York Diocese. Introduction by Dr Ronald Jasper.

In terms of specific hymn books, four are particularly useful for their subject indexes:

Hymns for Today's Church, 1982 (Sunday themes)

Hymns Ancient and Modern—New Standard Edition. 1983. (Hymns for the Sunday themes in the new lectionary.)

Hymns and Psalms. A Methodist and Ecumenical Hymn Book, 1983 (Liturgical Index)

The New English Hymnal. To be published in 1985.

Related books which will be useful as additional general guides include:

These are the Hymns, by Alan Dunstan. (SPCK) 1973.

Hymns and Tunes Indexed by first lines, tune names, and metres, by David W. Perry. (Hymn Society and RSCM) 1980.

and, in a general way, anything which deals with a hymn as a whole and provides material which a 'presenter' of hymns would find useful, e.g.

Hymns that Live, by Frank Colquhoun (Hodder and Stoughton) 1980.

Hymns for Today Discussed, by Cyril Taylor (Canterbury Press and RSCM) 1985.

Two words of warning. While a glance at the first verse may seem to make a certain hymn an ideal choice for a particular occasion, the remaining verses may prove less than suitable. Wedding couples often think of 'Through all the changing scenes of life' as reflecting suitable sentiments, which it does in the first verse. A glance at the remaining verses shows them to be less than apt. It is consequently important to consider a hymn *as a whole* before deciding on its suitability to a particular service or occasion.

Wedding hymns

While the choice here usually depends on whether the congregation consists for the most part of regular churchgoers or otherwise (and the latter will usually predominate), pages lxiii and lxiv of *A and M (NSE)*, together with the additional lists on pages lxvii and lxviii, give some indication of the amount of material now available in this book alone. Four examples, because they are out of the normal run, can be singled out for special consideration:

394. Lord of all hopefulness, Lord of all joy
450. Crown with love, Lord, this glad day
471. Holy Spirit, come, confirm us
475. Jesus, Lord, we pray

The end product

Whatever the final choice may ultimately be for any service and any situation, it is helpful to keep certain factors in mind, such as the essential need to think of the words first and the music second. In many minds the reverse too frequently obtains. How often the immediate reaction to a hymn is 'What a fine tune'; very seldom do we hear 'What magnificent words'. In the public estimation, hymns are more often than not judged first and foremost on the music, which anyhow is in many instances understandably more evocative than the text.

Then there is the importance of always having in mind the need to introduce new tunes. Released from music traditionally associated with the words and, when coupled to a different tune, the words usually take on an entirely new dimension and meaning. We all know 'Through the night of doubt and sorrow' to Martin Shaw's *Marching,* but link it to Parry's lesser known but no less fine *Rustington* (*A and M NSE* 211), and you have a completely different conception of the text, and something which Dykes' *St Oswald* never remotely achieves, even though this static tune has for many years been popularly associated with these words. It has certainly done little to carry the words a stage further, which is precisely what these other tunes do, and to admirable effect.

In a similar way, 'The Church of God a kingdom is' to *Crediton* (*A and M NSE* 502) and 'Praise the Lord! ye heavens, adore him' to Cyril Taylor's *Abbot's Leigh* (*A and M NSE* 356) provide fresh insights into the meaning of the words.

Likewise, the reverse can be equally revealing. Some of the many examples in *A and M (NSE)* which spring to mind where new words have been married to old tunes include:

335. A stranger once did bless the earth
358. Father, who in Jesus found us
361. For the healing of the nations
363. Glory to thee, O God
367. God of grace and God of glory
373. Help us, O Lord, to learn
379. Jesus, humble was your birth
395. Lord of all power, I give you my will
397. Lord, save thy world
403. Now let us from this table rise

407. O God in heaven, whose loving plan
410. O Holy Father, God most dear
415. Praise and thanksgiving
447. Christians, lift your hearts and voices
458. Forth in the peace of Christ we go

while among new tunes to old words are

170 (2nd tune) The Church's one foundation
87 (2nd tune) Hail the day that sees him rise
140 (2nd tune) All hail the power of Jesus' name!
172 (1st tune) Glorious things of thee are spoken
146 (2nd tune) When morning gilds the skies
254 (2nd tune) Thee we adore, O hidden Saviour, thee
306 (1st tune) How bright these glorious spirits shine!
324 (2nd tune) Give us the wings of faith to rise

When linking new tunes to old words it is important to bear in mind that the new tune be thought of as an alternative, and not always as a substitute, to what was familiarly associated with the words.

In the final count, it is once again the happy knack of finding what is right and what is wrong in the context of any particular service.

How many hymns do we need?

Taking into account all that has been previously said, we should in most situations think of not more than four hymns in any one service. This is especially applicable to the Parish Communion:

1. A good starter, ideally of not more than four or five verses. So as to set the scene, this needs to be a bright and vigorous hymn such as:

   1. Awake, my soul, and with the sun
   144. Come, let us join our cheerful songs
   207. Praise to the Lord, the almighty, the King of creation

427. The Son of God proclaim
446. Christians, lift up your hearts
483. Lift up your heads, you mighty gates

or a well known hymn applicable to a major festival.

2. Something contrasted, and short, for the Gradual:

    152. O Holy Spirit, Lord of grace
    373. Help us, O Lord, to learn
    448. Come, Holy Ghost, our hearts inspire
    491. Lord Jesus Christ, be present now

3. A longer, and more spacious, hymn for the Offertory. This is the place for those eight line verses mentioned earlier. The possibilities here are too numerous to mention individually.
4. A fairly short final hymn which sums up the service and which sends us out into the world in no uncertain way. The two A & M Supplements are particularly useful in this respect. (See also page 33.) Avoid, at all costs, as I recently encountered during Lent, 'Christian, dost thou see them'.

The same general principle will apply to Morning and Evening Prayer as to a special or free structured service.

If a hymn, or hymns, are to be sung at the communion of the people, this is an ideal moment for a choir to introduce new material as an anthem. If there is no choir these can be played instrumentally. Whichever way these are used, it is wise to tell the congregation, so that they can follow the new hymn in their books and thus become familiar with it prior to its being eventually sung in its own right during the course of a service.

This is also a suitable juncture for a short hymn anthem, such as one of John Wilson's simple arrangements of new hymns which are published in two books by the RSCM.*

**Sixteen Hymns of Today for use as simple anthems* and *Twenty-one Hymns, old and new, for use as simple anthems.*

In general terms, aim for around three-quarters of the hymns in most services being familiar, with the remainder being less well known. This introducing of new material is something which needs to be carefully programmed. As a rough guide, I would suggest this be not more than once a month. This allows continuity to the process. It is essential to sense the temperature and any feeling of resistance which in some churches makes it less easy to introduce new hymns than in others. It cannot be reiterated too forcibly that no two churches are alike either in tradition or needs, and that this will be reflected in the attitude of the congregation.

What can be achieved

A card index system containing every hymn in the book, or books, currently in use in one's church, is an invaluable guideline. If the date, together with the specific Sunday, festival or other occasion, is entered each time a hymn is sung, it will provide useful and sometimes revealing background information on the frequency with which certain examples are repeated as well as those seldom, or never, used.

Those of us in the Anglican Church need to take a metaphorical leaf out of the Free Church book. Because of the centrality of hymns which has always made them so basic and essential a musical constituent of Free Church services, they are almost without exception chosen with far more care than we Anglicans usually give to the matter.

Hymns and Psalms Log-Book, published by the Methodist Church Music Society, has been devised to encourage churches and preachers to record the hymns and psalms used in services, together with their frequency of use. Although the headings of the various sections would need to be adapted for Anglican use, the object of the exercise is to 'encourage full use of the wide selection of the material' contained in any hymn book.

Too often in the Anglican Church the choice is to a certain degree dictated by the reluctance of the clergy to be courageous. They too readily give in to 'we know what we like and we like what we know' attitudes from the pew.

In the end, it is all a matter of how you introduce, explain and 'sell' new hymns. Old dogs can be taught new tricks, but it is the way in which you go about it that matters.

Psalms as hymns

The constraints which result from the practical problems of singing the psalms, especially to Anglican chants, are leading more and more churches to abandon their use. This regrettable situation applies especially in those churches where there is either no choir or one with restricted resources, either of which does not allow full justice to be done to the exercise.

The growing realization that the psalms do not need to be sung exclusively to Anglican chants has led to various alternative, and easier, methods emerging in recent times. Notwithstanding, there are many hymns which are metrical versions of the psalms, and their appropriate use can do much to keep the spirit and the teaching of psalmody alive in those areas where traditional chanting may be impracticable.

In such instances the attention of the congregation needs to be drawn to the reason why a particular psalm, or its metrical version, is being used. Timothy Dudley-Smith's metrical version of Magnificat and Nunc Dimittis (*A and M NSE* 422 and 453), although well known, need to have far wider usage at Evening Prayer. How many people realize that, when they sing 'All people that on earth do dwell' or 'O worship the king', they are in fact singing metrical versions of Psalms 100 and 104. These are but two of the countless examples to be found in all the books. One of the greatest and finest of all metrical psalms is 'A safe stronghold our God is still' which, as traditionally sung to Luther's great melody *Ein feste Burg,* is none other than Psalm 46.

5
THE PRACTICALITIES OF CHOICE

With so many guidelines available nowadays to help us arrive at the right choice for any occasion, there is no excuse for the lame and uneventful menu which underlines much of what is heard Sunday by Sunday in many churches.

The options open to those whose task it is to select hymns makes it the more depressing in this enlightened age to be subjected, as many of us are, to such a narrow and 'safe' choice, the excuse for which is 'this is what the congregation want'. It would sometimes be more accurate to say that 'this is what the vicar likes, therefore . . .'.

This does not mean to say that all the clergy go about the choice of hymns in such a way. Many do take great trouble and consult with their organist and congregation in seeking to arrive at a choice which is, by consensus of agreement, acceptable to all parties. Such priests are wise and enlightened and they understand the significance of hymnody as a vital constituent of worship.

The advent of revised forms of service, together with new editions of hymn books or supplements to existing hymn books, have opened up an entirely new era and potential in hymnody which is both exciting and challenging. The extent of this is such as to have prompted Cyril Taylor to pose the question, 'Has the worldwide Church ever before experienced at any one time such a profusion of new material?'

A glance at some of the books mentioned in the Bibliography on page 96 gives some indication of what is now additionally available to help those whose task it is to choose hymns.

Because music as such, and hymns in particular, are both crucial and influential to all involved in any public worship situation, the dangers resulting from a confined and uneventful choice need to be the more emphasized and steps taken to avoid what will otherwise inevitably detract from a service. If a congregation is conservative in its ecclesiastical outlook, as many are, this is likely to surface prominently when it comes to hymns. Even so, it is the duty of those concerned to bring to the choice of hymns the insights which underline our new liturgies so that worship in all its rich components may potentially become the richer.

The positioning of hymns into any given service
(See also page 41)
While we may feel, and rightly so, that hymns are the one feasible way in which to involve a congregation musically, the simple fact is that in many instances there are too many hymns in our services. Using hymns to fill up otherwise awkward gaps is a blatant misuse of hymnody, as it is when they are employed in lieu of the moments of silence which worship today so frequently lacks.

In our all too often breathless pursuit of contemporary worship we have lost the ability to use silence. Many of us are frightened by silence, as witness the indiscriminate use of the television set, whether or not anyone happens to be looking at the screen. The assault on the ears of those who, as they move about in street or train wearing headphones connected to cassettes in their pockets, is a further example of our inability to cope with silence, to reject silence, even perhaps to fear it. Silence, when used aright, can be a rich attribute of worship. The problem is that in most instances, as compared with the contemplative orders of monasticism, we just do not know how to employ it.

Some clergy, moreover, subscribe to the belief that

the greater the number of hymns there are in a service, and especially if they are loud and fast, *ipso facto*, the better must be the end result, and the impact of the service. In reality, the sum total of hymns is surely of far less relevance than the right choice for the right occasion. This is what makes the lasting impression and increases the memorability of any church service.

Many churches now have a Parish Communion each Sunday. On most such occasions four hymns are ample, especially if carefully spaced out and used in the right places.

Among our new services, the Anglican Holy Communion Rite A gives a number of options in this respect, with the possible use of hymns at Sections 1, 16, 35, 47 and 50. Note, however, that no provision is made for a hymn *after* the dismissal, and for very good reasons.

For most purposes and occasions we are likely to need a hymn at the beginning, a second hymn at the offertory and another somewhere between the communion of the people and the end. A fourth hymn can be sung either at the gradual or during the administration of the Communion.

Alternatively, a psalm can sometimes be used, either sung or said, at the Gradual. There is much to be said for the weekly alternating of a psalm with a hymn. A further option is the singing of an anthem during the Communion. If there is no choir, the organ, an instrumental ensemble, or perhaps a gramophone record, could be usefully employed.

I mentioned just now how the position of the final hymn needs careful thought. This can become a controversial issue in Holy Communion Rite A and Rite B. The concept of a hymn as the grand finale of a service, and maybe sung as the choir moves towards the vestry, is a custom which dies hard in some churches. A hymn either during the ablutions, or *before* the dismissal, is surely preferable to being dismissed and then to back-track by singing a hymn. This makes a nonsense of the prayer in which we ask 'Send us out . . . to live and work to your praise and glory'. The dismissal must be the final statement emphasizing what we are going to do, which is to get out into the world and not to sing a hymn which will delay that process. If the organ starts immediately after the dismissal, then it is made the more real, even dramatic, and we are, as it were, propelled on our way.

At Morning or Evening Prayer three hymns—one at the start, with a second before the sermon, and the final hymn after it, are usually ample. These are services which, in the Book of Common Prayer version, are heavily loaded with psalms and canticles. Hymns therefore need to be reasonably minimal, especially at Matins.

The use of an office hymn is dealt with on page 86.

The custom of singing a hymn after the third collect merely breaks up the flow from structured prayer to intercessions and, for some unaccountable reason, does so in a way which does not happen if the choir sing an anthem at this point.

Those who choose hymns may frequently do so with care as to the actual choice but they do not always think a stage further as to the necessary variety needed in terms of key, mood and length, three important considerations which need to be continually borne in mind. It is all too easy to have two successive hymns in the same key, even in the same time, and certainly in the same mood. Always try to avoid two many hymns in long metre; they can be particularly dull, and wearisome to sing.

All of this can be avoided if, as mentioned earlier, clergy and organist choose the hymns together. This is a prime example of two heads being better than one.

Whatever service we have, there seems to be a firmly

entrenched belief that it must perforce begin with a hymn, often no doubt because it is felt that unless all concerned have 'a good sing' the service will not get under way as it should. From time to time in any situation, and certainly at a Parish Communion, an introit psalm can be a welcome alternative, provided you have a choir able to chant well. Nor is it irrelevant to bear in mind that Evensong in a cathedral will not on most occasions begin with a hymn.

Finally, I would suggest that if hymnody is to be used at the communion of the people, only one hymn be sung. The custom of filling up this juncture of the service, however long the communicating may take, with a succession of hymns which, more often than not, inevitably tend to jar against each other, musically and textually, is unjustifiable both liturgically and artistically. This is the more so if, when the celebrant is ready to move on to the next part of the service, the organist has been instructed to immediately end the hymn being sung. This not only mutilates a hymn but makes a nonsense of the text.

Worse still is the pernicious habit which still lingers on in some churches of singing a hymn twice or, where there is no choir, of the organist playing a miscellany of hymn tunes one after the other *ad infinitum.* These are gross abuses of hymnody and achieve nothing. There are always alternatives, such as the playing of suitable pieces, but not generally of improvising, a rare skill best reserved for the relatively few who are able to do so well. Few things are more offensive than the typical meandering or 'doodling' to which we are sometimes subjected.

The length of a hymn

This needs to be thought through in relation to what was said in Chapter 4. Some hymns are inordinately long and are tiring to sing, especially when, as in many instances, the pitch and consequent lie of the melodic line is too high for congregational singing. *Ancient and Modern Revised* number 400 is a particularly apt example, where in the Alleluias top F is far too high for most male voices, as for some ladies.

Eight-line verses can be particularly heavy weather. Easter and Harvest are occasions which seem particularly prone to having hymns of four, five or more, verses, each of eight lines (*AMR* 131, 132, 133, 137, 139, 482 and 484).

In an effort to combat these problems, some hymn books mark certain verses with a star, and these can be omitted without destroying anything essential to the overall sense or textual continuity. While this is in no way mandatory, it does help reduce the sheer bulk length. A careful study by clergy and musicians of hymns in this category can produce a sequence of verses which may be different on each occasion the hymn is used. It is thus more suited to the requirements of each and every service. Some hymns, such as 'Lift high the Cross', do not have an obvious sequence of thought, and this makes it easier to ring the changes. Conversely, 'Jesus, humble was your birth' (*A and M NSE* 379) and 'We have a gospel to proclaim' (*A and M NSE* 431) are instances where, because the sequence of thought takes us from the Incarnation to the Resurrection, all verses should be sung without exception.

Whatever the end product, I would emphasize the need to think out very carefully the rationale determining the omission of verses. A hasty and ill considered last minute decision in the vestry or, worse still, an off-the-cuff announcement during the course of a service—and this is by no means unknown—can produce diabolical and nonsensical results, such as omitting the final verse of 'Bright the vision that delighted'. To omit the final verse of a hymn will, in all but a very few instances, destroy the sense of the words. The final verse so often has the sting in the tail. 'When I survey the wondrous cross' is a case in point. To leave out such a verse is the same as not bothering to read the final chapter of a novel or a thriller.

Sensing the right length of a hymn for any given juncture in a service requires considerable care and thought. In any liturgical service, the readings, intercessions and sermon will, or should, reflect the theme of the day. Hymns, as I mentioned at the outset, come at regular intervals during the course of a service and, quite apart from their function, involve everyone musically. Carefully chosen hymns of the right length can do as much to highlight a service, as will inordinately long hymns, or too many hymns, nullify and contribute towards destroying the smooth flow in the sequence of events which underlies the memorability of a service. *I cannot emphasize this too much.*

If there is to be a hymn at the start of a service, it is generally best to have a short but lively one of not more than three or four verses. To sing five, or perhaps six, verses at this point weighs down the service instead of allowing it to move forward with a sense of purpose and momentum. The one exception to this would be if there is a large procession on a special occasion.

This initial hymn can act either as an introit ('Come, let us join our cheerful songs' is a good starter for a Parish Communion) or, at Mattins, 'Christ, whose glory fills the skies'. The short version of 'O come, all ye faithful' is an obvious starter for Christmas Day.

A reflective, slow or soft hymn, or perhaps one in a minor key, will not necessarily act as a mood setter nor impel the service on its way. 'All ye who seek for comfort sure' is, to my way of thinking, a far better starter to the first Sunday in Lent than 'Forty days and forty nights', which inevitably seems to herald this season. It will have more impact and better effect elsewhere.

If, in a Parish Communion service, there is to be a Gradual hymn, it should be a short one, such as 'O Holy Spirit, Lord of Grace', otherwise the natural sequence from Epistle to Gospel will be thrown out of balance. A hymn, or psalm, at this particular juncture should act merely as a musical bridge. The two supplements to *Hymns A and M* purposely include a number of suitable examples:

15. Come, Lord, to our souls come down
40. Help us, O Lord, to learn
59. Lord Jesus, once you spoke to men
84. Praise we now the Word of grace
90. Thanks to God whose Word was spoken (a fine example, though a shade long)

100 Hymns for Today also cites further hymns under the heading of 'The Good News':

32. God is Love; let heav'n adore him
36. God who created this Eden of earth
89. Tell out, my soul, the greatness of the Lord
98. We have a gospel to proclaim

More Hymns for Today earmarks eight hymns as being specially suitable for the Gradual:

105. Can man by searching find out God
115. Come, Holy Ghost, our hearts inspire
134. God, who hast caused to be written thy word
135. God, who spoke in the beginning
157. Lord, I have made thy word my choice
158. Lord Jesus Christ, be present now
176. Rise and hear! The Lord is speaking
180. The prophets spoke in days of old

Here are nearly a score of comparatively new hymns, all with an emphasis on musically leading in to the Gospel.

The hymn at the Offertory ought to be of sufficient

length to cover the celebrant doing the preparation which is necessary at the altar, the taking of the collection and its delivery to the altar. In some churches there will also be the presenting of the elements. Too short a hymn will result in either of two generally undesirable things, the organist improvising before or after the final verse of the hymn or the repetition of certain verses merely to avoid the silence which is so feared in many churches.

Because the congregation on Christmas Day and at Easter is likely to be far greater in number than on an average Sunday, the offertory hymn on these occasions should be longer than for a normal Sunday.

Some of us have reservations about the singing of a hymn while the collection is being made. The Free Churches usually collect the offertory during the playing of organ music. This procedure is commonplace in many United States churches and is followed by the singing of the doxology ('Praise God, from whom all blessings flow') at its conclusion.

In most churches the hymns at Evensong tend to be shorter than those used in the mornings. As congregations are often much smaller in the evening, two, or at the most, three, hymns would seem to be ample. As to where in the service these hymns are sung is another matter and something which will be decided according to local custom.

Alternative tunes and what they can achieve

For many of us, words and tunes are indissolubly wedded through familiarity and have been ever since we were weaned. It is inconceivable, almost to the point of heresy, to imagine 'Abide with me' and 'Onward, Christian soldiers' being sung to anything but the tune we all know.

With the advent of so many excellent new tunes there is surely every incentive to use them as alternatives—which does not mean substitutes—to those generally associated with certain words. Some, such as *North Petherton* to 'Come down, O love divine' and Stanford's *Engleberg* to 'For all the saints' were used in *A and M Revised*, this because Vaughan Williams' *Down Ampney* and *Sine nomine* were unobtainable because of copyright restrictions. This has been rectified in the New Standard Edition.

When a text is linked with a new and less familiar tune it serves to make us sit up and think in a new way about the meaning of those words.

'Praise to the holiest' has always had two tunes, *Gerontius* and *Richmond*, inseparably associated with it. Both are to be found in *A and M Revised* and in the New Standard Edition. A third tune, *Somervell*, is also included. As a fourth, R. R. Terry's magnificent *Billing* (New Standard Edition) is suggested. This is fine, bold and striding music set to Isaac Watts' 'Lord, I have made thy word my choice' (490 in the New Standard Edition).

Is it too much to suggest that all four tunes be used in rotation for a hymn which is so frequently used? A similar marrying up of the first two of these tunes is also possible for 'City of God'.

Cyril Taylor's *Abbot's Leigh* is cast in a frequently used metre (87.87.D). Because of its unique and never failing qualities it has not surprisingly become one of the most popular tunes of our time. A glance at the index of hymns in this metre will show how apt it is for a number of situations.

In my last book, *Church Music in a Changing World* (Mowbray), I mentioned a number of possible alternatives, such as what I believe to be the dullness of the tune *Aurelia* and how it positively detracts from the strength of 'The Church's one foundation'. Link these words with Vaughan Williams' *King's Lynn* (New Standard Edition 170) and you immediately come up with an entirely new concept and dimension. I am told that when Mervyn Stockwood was Bishop of Southwark he used Elgar's 'Land of hope and glory' tune to the words 'At the name of Jesus'. It may, on the face of it, seem a strange marriage, but it works; the two fit like a glove to the hand and, what is more, complement each other.

These are but a few examples and, even if outstanding ones, I would suggest that whenever good alternative tunes suggest themselves we ring the changes, if only for the sake of variety.

The 'casual' service

Up till now we have been considering the choice of hymns for use in structured and familiar liturgical services where their function and place are generally well defined and understood. The choice, and use, of hymns for special or occasional services is more difficult. There are a number of understandable reasons why this is so, not least that hymns on such occasions have a more significant, and certainly functional, role to play. The rightness of choice is therefore crucial.

The often conservative views and the restricted knowledge of hymnody of those who are not regular churchgoers are a contributory factor which has to be taken into account, if not necessarily always heeded in the event. The wishes of those to be married or those responsible for funeral arrangements will frequently be dictated by sentiment and nostalgia or will find an outlet in music associated with current 'hits' or evangelical hymns and choruses, all of this simply because the musical experience of those concerned is probably limited to these less than appropriate areas.

Traditionally orientated organists are sometimes understandably resentful when asked to perform music cast in a style and mould which is not their normal scene and, moreover, are expected to play such music on the organ, an instrument far removed from what such music was probably conceived for. The resulting constraints can be formidable.

The music, canned or otherwise, likely to be encountered at crematoria does not strictly come within the terms of my brief. Nevertheless, this is a particularly vulnerable area where the pros and cons of suitable hymnody are especially likely to be encountered, and in a somewhat controversial way. Once again, the ethics of what many of us would consider to be suitable are likely to be outweighed here by popular demand or what the crematorium has on offer on its current cassette, a choice which will probably leave much to be desired.

In terms of specific services I would suggest—but stress that this is only a suggestion—some of what I believe to be both suitable and relevant for the general needs of the 1980s. What follows includes in the main some of the new material in the two *A and M* supplements. Numbers refer to *A and M NSE:*

Baptism:

342. Awake, awake, fling off the night
343. Be thou my vision
348. Come, Lord, to our souls come down
374. Help us to help each other, Lord
376. In Christ there is no east or west
402. Now is eternal life
445. Christians, lift up your hearts
452. Eternal God, we consecrate
466. God the Father, name we treasure
506. Praise and thanksgiving be to our Creator
521. We praise you, Lord

There is a further and comprehensive selection under the heading of 'Holy Baptism' on page lxvii of the New Standard Edition of *A and M.*

Marriage:

In addition to four newer hymns mentioned in passing

in Chapter 4 (page 39), other possible choices which could be slotted in around the more familiar examples likely to be asked for, include:

356. Father, Lord of all Creation
374. Help us to help each other, Lord
378. Jesus, good above all other
379. Jesus, humble was your birth
380. Jesus, Lord, we look to thee
393. Lord of all good, our gifts we bring to thee
459. Give me joy in my heart
476. Jesus, my Lord, let me be near you
503. Of all the Spirit's gifts to me

These come from the two supplements of *A and M* which now form the latter part of the New Standard Edition. A further list of the more familiar marriage hymns can be found on pages lxvii and lxviii of the same edition.

Funerals:

Obvious choices here are to be found under the heading of 'Funeral and Commemoration' on page lxviii of the New Standard Edition. There is a further selection in the two supplements. These are too many to quote individually but can be found in the subject index under:

God–His providence,
Hope,
Jesus Christ–crucified and risen.

I would however specifically mention four as being especially worthy of consideration in general terms:

82. Jesus lives!
110. The God of love my shepherd is
428. Thine be the glory, risen, conquering Son
453. Faithful vigil ended

Civic occasions:

With this could be coupled the section headed 'National' in books such as *EH* and *SP.* From *A and M*

NSE there are:

346. Christ is the world's true light (to *Nun danket*)
353. Eternal Ruler of the ceaseless round
355. (part 2) Father all-loving, thou rulest in majesty
361. For the healing of the nations
396. Lord of lords and King eternal (to *Rhuddlan* or *Regent Square*)
405. O day of God, draw nigh
409. O Holy City, seen of John. (Although Herbert Howells' splendid *Sancta Civitas* was written for these words, it is not a good congregational tune. It will be best sung to a familiar common metre tune with the second half repeated.)
432. What does the Lord require (this metre has no familiar tune)
483. Lift up your heads, you mighty gates
522. We turn to you, O God of every nation

Remembrance and other commemorations, including Battle of Britain

Hymns are always suggested in any of the official Orders of Service for Remembrance. Other obvious sources would be Easter, Dedication, World Peace and the 'Service of Others'. 'O God, our help in ages past', although inevitable, is nevertheless a fine hymn which has much to commend in it.

Flower Festivals and the Arts in general

104. For the beauty of the earth
116. All things bright and beautiful
199. Immortal, invisible, God only wise
202. Let all the world in every corner sing
204. Let us, with a gladsome mind

SP is the one book where the index of *Hymns arranged for Sundays and other days throughout the year* ranges widest, especially into the arena of flower and arts festivals, together with other such 'non churchy' occasions.

As mentioned in Chapter 1 it is important to be constantly widening the choice and range of hymns, the more so as so much good new material is now available. Where weddings and funerals are concerned, I suggest that clergy and organists encourage the slotting in of a less familiar example, having first explained—and this is crucial—why such and such a hymn is being proposed and how its text is eminently suitable for the occasion.

In a similar way, while it would be generally unthinkable to omit certain well established favourites at Christmas, Easter and Harvest, it is possible, and highly desirable, to ring the changes sometimes by including hymns which may be less familiar or even entirely new. If we are content with a virtually exclusive diet of the old favourites we shall never progress, let alone break new ground. Nor must we forget that 'Onward, Christian soldiers' and 'Abide with me' were at one time new and probably entirely suspect, even resented. There is an interesting parallel here with the hostile reception which some of the music of Brahms and Wagner received, music which nowadays could not sound more easy on the ears.

In recommending hymns, any selection must be both arbitrary and therefore to an extent personal. While recognizing this, I append some lesser known alternatives which are well worth study and careful presentation to a congregation. As before, these come from the New Standard Edition of *A and M:*

Christmas:

44. Behold, the great Creator makes himself a house of clay
45. To us a Child of royal birth
511. The great Creator of the worlds
527. Where is this stupendous stranger?

(What a superb first line. Have you ever thought of the infant Christ as such? The author of these fine words was Christopher Smart, an eighteenth century priest who spent much of his life in a mental home. It was his unusual text which Benjamin Britten used for *Rejoice in the Lamb.*)

Lent:

57. My spirit longs for thee
351. Creator of the earth and skies
368. God of love and truth and beauty
(A fine hymn which illustrates the Lord's Prayer)
397. Lord, save thy world
472. How shall I sing that majesty
492. Lord of all, to whom alone all our hearts' desires are known

Easter:

437. Away with gloom, away with doubt
443. Christian people, raise your song
479. Let the Lord's People, heart and voice uniting

Harvest:

370. God, whose farm is all creation
415. Praise and thanksgiving, Father, we offer
457. For the fruits of his creation
486. Lord, by whose breath all souls and seeds are living

Advent is already fully catered for and has one of the most wide ranging and comprehensive choices available for any one season of the Church's year. Pentecost is another matter, with few of the standard hymn books having much to provide for what is one of the Church's three major festivals. The two *A and M* supplements have made a significant contribution in catering for this deficiency and include a number of new hymns relevant to the Holy Spirit.

To summarize, I cannot over-emphasize the dangers which in each and every separate situation can arise either from repetitiveness or from the small range of choice which sometimes underlies not only the week by week diet but equally the major festivals. It is the predictability, the uneventfulness (which sometimes includes the way in which hymns are played and sung) and the lack of any sense of exploration in taking up what is currently available, which can combine to produce what in many instances is a depressing feature of worship today. The sad thing is that while this of necessity reacts on choir and congregation, who will readily complain among themselves, no one usually registers any such complaint with the clergy.

I have often quoted that very useful verse from the Book of Proverbs—'Where there is no vision, the people perish'. One could equally say that where there is vision, then there is life. This is applicable as much to hymns as to anything else.

6
PRACTICALITIES OF PERFORMANCE

By and large, we are very often guilty of lack of vision over the way in which we sing and play hymns. This all too often results in sounds which are pedestrian, routine, and consequently dull and uneventful. Musicians sometimes offload their responsibility towards hymns, viewing them as a relatively unimportant aspect of their work. So it is not to be wondered at that something which, in a unique way is totally inclusive in that it involves all taking part in a worship situation, all too frequently falls short of the ideal it should present and, by no means least, the impact it should make.

In my experience, I find that many church musicians are surprisingly blinkered on this subject and that, consequently, they neither appreciate the importance of hymnody nor in any way concentate on what should be the priority of its presentation.

The individuality of hymns

A wide variety of styles, mood and musical content mean that in an ideal situation no two hymns are, or should be, alike. In practice, hymns in the course of a service are more often than not subjected to a sameness of identity and performance which irons out any individual personality and which can result in a uniformity of sound which is both dull and pedestrian. What opportunities are therefore missed, and what a disservice is done to the cause of hymnody which, when chosen and used aright, can project such variety and contrast.

Hymns fall into a wide range of categories, and do so for a number of reasons. It must suffice here to mention the main groupings.

1. Those with strong and positive texts which are carried a stage further by a bright, striding, and briskly moving tune allied to straightforward harmonies. Such hymns have an onward rhythmic thrust and fit almost anywhere within the context of most general purpose services and especially if taken at a good speed. These include examples such as:

   Ye holy angels bright
   Bright the vision
   Ye servants of God
   Ye choirs of new Jerusalem

2. Hymns which, although they possess many of the qualities just mentioned, move in a more legato and spacious way:

   All glory, laud and honour
   Father, Lord of all creation
   Ye that know the Lord is gracious
   Praise to the Lord, the Almighty

3. Hymns which are reflective in mood and where the music partners this. Such examples need to be sung quietly and at a correspondingly gentle tempo:

   Blest are the pure in heart
   Jesu, lover of my soul (when sung to *Hollingshead*)
   Faithful shepherd, feed me
   Jesus, humble was your birth

4. Some hymns come mid-way between and within these three categories. They are consequently harder to pigeon-hole and each needs careful thought in deciding on the ideal interpretation:

O worship the King
There is a land of pure delight
Children of the heavenly king
Come down, O love divine

5. Hymns which are fast moving and have an almost military two or four-in-a-bar precision:

We plough the fields and scatter
Tell out, my soul, the greatness of the Lord
Firmly I believe and truly (when sung to *Halton Holgate*)
Love's redeeming work is done

6. Hymns which need a musically broad and sustained treatment, both because of the words themselves and because of the presence of a number of passing notes in the tune:

Jesu, lover of my soul (to *Aberystwyth*)
Praise the Lord, rise up rejoicing (*A and M NSE* 416)
For the healing of the nations (to *Tantum ergo*)
King of glory, King of peace

7. Certain examples have the variety of some verses, or parts of verses, in unison while others are in harmony. The latter nearly always call for a more sustained and richer legato treatment as compared with a more striding and potent rhythm in the verses for unison voices. Examples in this category include:

For all the saints (to Vaughan Williams' *Sine nomine*)
Lift high the cross
Ye watchers and ye holy ones
Good Christian men, rejoice and sing (to *Gelobt sei Gott*)

These are but some of the definitives which can be offered as guidelines. One could go on for ever categorizing and making suggestions, though every example needs to be thought through in its own right. Suffice it to say that certain general pointers should always determine the musical considerations:

1. *The shape of the tune.* A good tune has an onward thrust which provides its energy and impetus. Many hymn tunes, as with Anglican chants, gradually build up towards a climax which usually occurs towards the end. *Richmond* (*A and M NSE* 125) will suffice as a case in point. Here the highest melodic note comes at the end of the third quarter of the tune and it is the more heightened by the modulation to the dominant key (C major) which precedes this.

2. *The words and the tune.* Do they marry satisfactorily, and does the music add to the realization of the words? Or does the tune detract from the text? Does it perhaps take over from the text? There are plenty of examples where a poor text would (or should) have long since disappeared were it not for the tune which saves it. 'Jerusalem, my happy home' is, to my way of thinking, not a very good text, but sing it to *Southwell*, as in *A and M NSE* 187, and the words are given a new lease of life.

   In a reverse way, a good text has sometimes been saddled to poor music. Such is 'Lead, kindly Light, amid the encircling gloom' where Dykes' tune *Lux benigna* is for ever stopping and starting and does little to suggest the onward movement underlying the mood of the words. This defect is happily remedied by William Harris's fine tune *Alberta* which has all the sense of movement which Dykes completely missed out on.

   A further exceedingly happy marriage of words and tune is that of Cyril Taylor's *Abbots Leigh* when linked with Stuart Cross's fine words 'Father, Lord of all Creation' (*A and M NSE* 356) or 'Ye that know the Lord is gracious' when sung to *Hyfrydol* (*A and M NSE* 175).

3. *Tempo and dynamics.* These need to be related and adapted to the size of a building, the numbers singing, and whether the choir, congregation and organ are relatively near each other or are at a distance.

   A further practicality which should determine pace is that pure melody (i.e. a unison tune) can move faster, with more flexibility and less restriction than a harmonized (SATB) tune, which needs to be more expansive.

   Tunes in triple time can all too easily sound lethargic and waltz-like. 'The day thou gavest, Lord, is ended', 'Be thou my guardian and my guide' and 'Praise to the Lord, the Almighty, the King of creation' will be all but ruined, and grossly misinterpreted, if sung in such a way. Triple time can have great strength.

   Most of the recent hymn books omit dynamics from the words. This helps to avoid the sentimental approach which for generations seemed to dictate that anything to do with death was automatically pianissimo, while mention of nails and piercing in Passiontide hymns called for the use of swell reeds. A broader and less fussy overall approach is now being generally adopted and is far more effective than bland attempts at word painting, though it is remarkable to witness the speed with which some organists manage to change stops at such moments.

   Similarly, not every hymn should necessarily end with choir and organ fortissimo. *A and M NSE* 450, 453 and 503 are but three such examples.

4. Having carefully considered the mood and character of each and every hymn in any given service and, not least, the relationship of one hymn to

another through juxtaposition, all that remains is to sing and accompany each and every example to advantage. This, I hasten to add, demands constant thought and preparation together with a continual reassessment of one's critical faculties.

An over-riding consideration must always be the need to put across the rhythmic considerations of any hymn. While this is obviously mandatory and basic to all music, it is the more essential in hymns, where so many tunes move in notes of more or less equal value.

In terms of the music, it will greatly help if in quadruple time the second and fourth beats are lightened: $\underline{1}$ $\underset{\cdot}{2}$ $\underline{3}$ $\underset{\cdot}{4}$ and in triple time the second and third beats likewise: $\underline{1}$ $\underset{\cdot}{2}$ $\underset{\cdot}{3}$. In many instances the verbal accentuation will mirror this. Careful note of these two factors, which are of course complementary, will result in a rhythmic lilt as opposed to the plodding sounds all too frequently experienced. 'Praise the Lord, rise up rejoicing' (*A and M NSE* 416) is as good an example as any of this need.

In general, if you *think* in terms of two in a bar instead of four, and one in a bar instead of three, this will in almost every instance be an additional rhythmic help.

The importance of the organ introduction

The function of what is familiarly termed 'the play-over' is two-fold: Firstly, it acts as a reminder of the tune. This has an especially practical consideration nowadays when new alternatives to the familiar 'old favourites' are frequently being used.

Secondly, the play-over can, and should, suggest a lot more in addition. It must indicate the tempo; therefore, any rallentando at the end of the play-over, or any shortening or lengthening of the final chord, destroys the tempo and rhythm which has been established. For similar reasons it is essential that the hymn itself is played at *exactly* the same speed as was the introduction, and that the congregation are not allowed to drag.

The responsibility for the successful and convincing performance of any hymn is therefore vested in how the organist introduces that hymn.

The function of the play-over should, in its short space, also suggest the character and broad dynamic of the hymn. It would be as unhelpful to introduce 'O come, all ye faithful' on swell strings as it would be to preface 'Abide with me' with full organ.

The mood and character of any hymn will surely determine whether its introduction should be loud, soft, legato or otherwise.

The length of the play-over, moreover, needs to be carefully thought out in advance. One or two lines of a verse will suffice, the better still when this ends on the dominant chord or key, with the tune commencing on the tonic chord:

'The King of love my shepherd is' (Tune: *Dominus regit me–A and M NSE* 126)

'When I survey the wondrous Cross' (Tune: *Rockingham–A and M NSE* 67)

The singing of a hymn such as 'Ye holy angels bright' to *Darwall's 148th* prefaced by the first six notes played loudly in octaves, in strict time and with the right hand slightly detached, can be a memorable and exciting sound guaranteed to make a choir and congregation respond in no uncertain way.

A tune such as *Luckington* can benefit from a special type of introduction consisting of the first four chords followed by the final four chords. This, however, is an exception and will only come off effectively in a very few instances.

The American custom of playing the entire tune as an introduction, irrespective of its length, is a tedious process and seems to me to induce the very reverse of activating the singers. Equally infuriating is the habit of playing as the introduction the final few bars of a tune. We surely recognize any tune by its start and not necessarily by its ending.

The play-over should never be a mundane or routine matter. Handled aright, it will suggest a lot which is essential if the hymn is to sound convincing. These considerations apply even more to the opening hymn in a service, for this determines to a great extent the impetus, or otherwise, of all that follows. What an influence the organist wields in this respect.

Key

When *Hymns Ancient and Modern* first appeared in 1861 it was intended for four part SATB choirs. The choice of key therefore aimed to reflect the general overall range and comfort of all four voice parts. Congregational singing is prevalent today in a way unknown or envisaged a century ago. This means that many of the hymns, even in *A and M Revised*, are pitched too high for congregations singing in unison. Some tunes are particularly awkward in that their melodic spread is so wide. *Darwall's 148th* ('Ye holy angels bright') and *St Helen* ('Lord, enthroned in heavenly splendour') are two instances which will present problems in this respect, whatever key is used.

The New Standard Edition of *A and M* took the plunge and transposed many of the tunes into lower keys. While this did much to placate congregations, it was bad news for choirs who now find the lie of some of the inner parts too low for comfort. It is one of those situations where it is impossible to please one party without upsetting the other. Even with the lower keys used in *NSE*, men in the congregation continue to growl approximate sounds which are usually well below the note.

For most congregational purposes the extremes of

pitch ought not to exceed treble D at the top and lower middle B flat at the other end.

Perhaps Elizabeth Poston hit on a compromise in her treatment of *St Ethelwald* ('Soldiers of Christ, arise') in *The Cambridge Hymnal*. Here, each successive verse modulates into a key a semitone higher than the preceding one. The hymn commences in E flat and, after six verses, ends in A flat.

In general terms there are also other considerations concerning the choice of key, all of them practical and environmental, such as, for example, the first hymn at a morning service being pitched too high. Similarly, undue heating in a church can upset the pitch.

Amens

These are seldom used nowadays apart from the custom in some churches when the final verse happens to be a doxology. As with the Gloria sung at the end of a psalm, we have an ascription of praise to the Trinity. Both, by long tradition, conclude with an Amen.

The custom of slowing down and getting softer is a sentimental habit best avoided. If Amen is to be sung it should be both rhythmic and in strict time, thus keeping up the momentum and adding something positive:

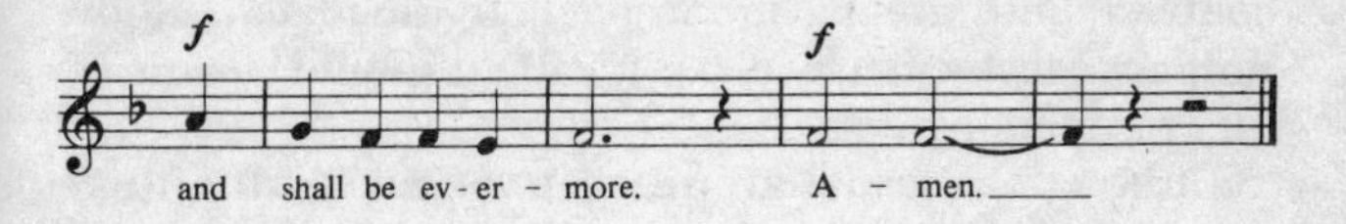

with the rest neatly observed as a point of punctuation.

Descants

At one time these were very popular, certainly with choirs. Nowadays, when congregations play a more prominent role in the singing of hymns, the use of descants in tending to become more of a rarity. They can also act as a distraction to congregational singing.

The more traditional examples, such as 'O worship the King' and 'Ye holy angels bright' in *A and M Revised*, are often the most satisfactory, as are the Willcocks descants in the two books of *Carols for Choirs* (OUP). Some of these, although they have become the more familiar through their association with the annual Christmas Eve carol service from King's College, Cambridge, are splendidly majestic examples in their own right. Into this category come 'Once in royal David's city' and 'Hark! the herald-angels sing', with 'O come, all ye faithful' probably the finest of all, being carried a stage further by the splendid free harmonization written for the final verse.

More recently, some composers have elected to write descants which commence after the main tune has started and therefore overlap or dovetail the ends of the lines, such as John Wilson's example for his tune *Lauds*(*A and M NSE* 515) and the Willcocks' descant for 'It came upon the midnight clear' (*Carols for Choirs* Book 2).

Sopranos and trebles understandably enjoy singing descants, but their use must not result in a shouting match between all concerned. A descant, because it is a complementary tune sung by high voices, will always be easily heard in its own right. It is therefore in marked contrast, both tonally and in pitch, to the main melody sung usually by men's voices. Ideally, it should be a fifty-fifty partnership.

Although descants are often reserved for the final verse of a hymn or, as in 'Bright the vision', for the third and final verses, there is surely no restriction on their being used for any verse, providing the words call for a special treatment. Nor need descants always be sung. They can be equally effective when played on the organ, and even more so if a trumpeter is available.

Free organ harmonizations

When done well—and it must be conceded that relatively few organists are capable of this—these can add much to the dimension of a hymn.

In less than capable hands they are best left alone, thus avoiding embarrassment for all concerned, not least to the player when it all goes wrong and comes off the rails. In the right hands free harmonizations can be a memorable enrichment and uplift, the more so when done in a less than flamboyant way. It merely needs a few salient chord variants and the rethinking of moves towards the cadence points.

A number of books are in existence which do it for you. The best examples are the work of undisputed experts in the field. Such collections include *Accompaniments for Unison Hymn Singing* (RSCM) and *Last Verse in Unison*, a particularly interesting and discerning collection of twenty-four well known hymn tunes arranged by Harrison Oxley. This is also published by the RSCM.

As with descants, free harmonizations do not always need to be reserved for the final verse.

There is also a particularly fine collection published in 1912 by Clowes for *Hymns Ancient and Modern*. Some of the examples may be somewhat flamboyant or extravagant though one in particular, by Charles Macpherson, is very fine. It provides three variants for the hymn 'Bright the vision'. The collection is unfortunately out of print as is a similar collection by Bairstow which was published by OUP.

Harmonies

For reasons which we need not go into here, and which mainly concern the vagaries of copyright, certain harmonizations have until recently been restricted in their potential use in that they were available only in certain hymn books.

The *A and M Revised* harmonies for *Hyfrydol* are cumbersome and awkward as compared with *EH* 301. This has now been rectified in *A and M NSE* 262. 'Praise, my soul, the King of heaven' is another example which invites comparison between *A and M* and *EH,* while *Lasst uns erfreuen* ('Ye watchers and ye holy ones') is on every count to be recommended in the *EH* 519 version. The *AMR* version is by contrast stilted and awkward, and consequently lacking in flow. This also has been remedied in the *NSE.*

Many such anomalies have been put to rights since copyright restrictions have in recent times been lifted and the consequent exchange of material made very much easier for all concerned.

Pauses in chorales

These were included by Bach and others purely and simply to indicate the ends of lines. Even so, there are mixed views on whether or not the pause marks should be observed. As a result of divided opinions on this, and the fact that the pause sign is one of the most indeterminate of musical indications in that it can be interpreted in virtually any way, it is probably best if in hymns these are ignored. In any event, they hold up the flow in tunes such as *Wachet auf* and *Ein' feste Burg* where each line is generally quite short in length.

Whatever is decided on, and if they are observed, their length must be consistent and rhythmic, with care taken over words ending in a consonant and where an extra beat needs to be added for the cut-off and for taking breath. 'Now thank we all our God' (*A and M NSE* 205) is an example where, at the end of the second line of words, an extra beat needs to be inserted for breathing:

A somewhat similar example is 'Glory to thee, my God, this night'. Here, at the end of the second line of words, although an extra beat as such may not be called for, time must be given for the singers to breath. An element of give and take should therefore pertain. The main consideration here, as elsewhere, is to avoid impeding the natural and rhythmic flow of the music.

A novel exception, and for entirely different reasons, comes in the third verse of 'Jesus Christ is risen today'. When Sir Edward Bairstow was organist of York Minster he introduced a broad rallentando at the words 'Now above the sky he's King' which included three beats on the word 'King' followed by a beat rest. This point of emphasis was most effective and became part of the York tradition. But, for general purposes, the introduction of something such as this can only be entirely effective when the congregation are warned in advance, and told the reasons why.

Gaps between verses

The same principles apply here as for pauses in that they must be consistent and rhythmic. Organists often seem oblivious of the fact that singers have to be allowed ample time to breathe at the ends of verses and that sometimes an element of give and take must obtain at the ends of lines, especially where the tidiness of final consonants is concerned.

If the spaces between the verses are rhythmically and consistently thought out, the singers will soon follow suit. If there is no choir, the organist must be especially careful and disciplined in this respect. On no account should these gaps be determined by the time needed for manipulating stop changes.

In 'Praise to the holiest' when sung to *Richmond*, the last note of the verse has three beats. This means that the final consonant comes on the next beat which should be followed by two silent beats in *strict* time:

A similar example is 'Praise, my soul, the King of heaven':

In tunes which begin on the up-beat it is sometimes better, and certainly more rhythmic, to add an extra beat. Take as an example 'O praise ye the Lord' as sung to *Laudate Dominum:*

Two points need to be especially emphasized and constantly borne in mind:

1. A beat must always be given its full value and consequently lasts until the next beat commences. This necessitates the final consonant being sounded at the beginning of the next beat. Three beats on the word 'God' is

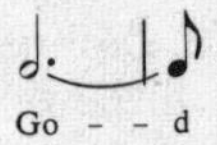

For those who cannot work this one out, the parallel is that if you walk three miles, the end of the third mile will coincide with the precise moment that the fourth mile commences—and not before.

2. In order that rhythmic continuity can be achieved, the final note of a hymn tune will in practice sometimes need to be shortened in length. *Franconia* ('Blest are the pure in heart') is a good example of this. If the final note is a minim and not a dotted minim, the rhythmic continuity will be better.

One of the practical problems is that when we rehearse hymns we usually take each verse on its own and then perhaps stop to make a point about what has just been sung. The continuity from one verse to another is thus seldom rehearsed and only becomes a reality when we sing the hymn straight through at a service.

A further obstacle to rhythmic continuity occurs when an organist elects to hold on to the final chord, instead of releasing the chord with the singers.

Gathering notes or 'door knockers'

At one time it was an almost universal custom for the organ to hold the first chord of each verse until the singers decided to come in. Although this is not yet completely a thing of the past, it is far less in evidence today, and for very good reasons. It is not a habit to be encouraged as it holds up the rhythmic flow of the music and creates an element of uncertainty and a resulting untidiness of attack. If, as mentioned just now, the gaps between verses are consistent, all concerned will quickly adapt to the habit of coming in with the organ, and not after it.

I inherited a 'door knocker' tradition when I became organist of Exeter Cathedral but, when I made the decision to abandon this, the new approach was smoothly operative within two or three weeks, with the resultant singing of choir and congregation far more lively and orderly.

Phrasing

Although this is a necessary ingredient of any intelligent

verbal or vocal utterance, in church music, and especially in the singing and playing of hymns, it is frequently either ignored or merely accorded casual lip service.

If every word or syllable is given identical stress the result will inevitably be extremely dull, and unrelenting hard work.

In addition, we have to bear in mind that hymn tunes in the main consist of a succession of unremitting four parts chords, many of which are of equal duration. A literal interpretation can frequently result in something bordering on the bizarre, especially in terms of failing to match the musical and rhythmic implications of the words and the music. A line such as 'Blest are the pure in heart' can all too easily become 'Blest | *are* the *pure* in | *heart*' instead of '*Blest* are the *pure*
4 1 2 3 4 1
in *heart*'. Here, the first note of the tune is on the weakest (fourth) beat of the bar, yet this coincides with the strong verbal accent needed on 'Blest'.

Similarly, the fourth verse of 'How sweet the name of Jesus sounds',
'Je | sus! my Shep-herd, | Brother, Friend'
4 1 2 3 4 1 2 3
is yet another instance where the normal rhythmic stresses of the music have to take second place to the needs and sense of the words, and where the initial upbeat word or syllable has to be stressed instead of lightened. A glance through any hymn book will reveal many such instances where textual sense takes precedence over normal musical rhythms.

Linked with this are further considerations vital to the intelligent singing and playing of hymns. By no means every line ends with a punctuation mark, nor does the sense of the words always call for this. Yet congregations—and sometimes choirs—almost invariably take a breath at the end of each line and in doing so ruin the word sense. This is an ingrained habit, probably accentuated by the fact that the ends of lines frequently coincide with long musical notes.

Most recent hymn books include a slur ‿ at the end of those lines where the phrasing of the words carries over to the next line. The same principle applies in hymns with short lines, e.g. 'Ye holy angels bright' and 'Lord of the worlds above' (*A and M NSE* 165). In such instances where lines need to be joined up, a slight crescendo of intensity will help:

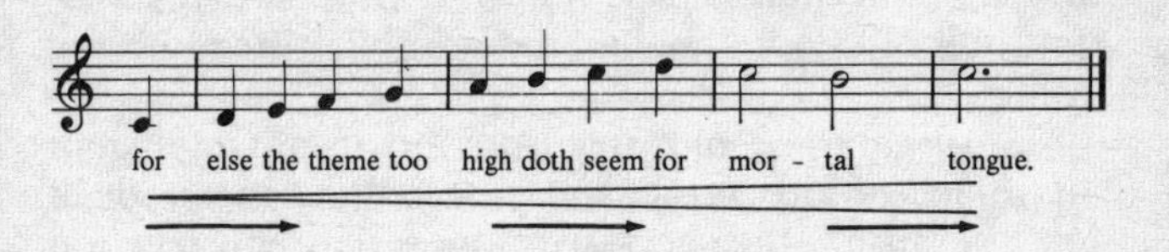

In a related way, certain phrases need careful and deliberate phrasing. Chestnuts such as 'My God, I love thee not because' and 'Thy kingdom come on bended knee' are all too frequently sung as one phrase without thought for the punctuation, although a breath will invariably be taken at the end of the line. This utterly destroys the word sense of what should be 'Thy kingdom come! on bended knee the passing ages pray' and 'My God, I love thee; not because I hope for heaven thereby'. In both instances, there needs to be a clearly articulated gap after the exclamation mark or semicolon, in order to convey the impact of the initial phrase, after which the remainder of that line and the next line should be sung in one breath.

In the fourth verse of 'How sweet the name of Jesus sounds', while we ought to ignore the exclamation mark and the commas, an accent or stress on the word or the main syllable will achieve the required result:

'<u>Je</u> – sus! my <u>Shepherd</u>, <u>Bro</u>ther, <u>Fri</u>end'

A useful golden rule is to think in terms of as few main beats in the bar as possible. This applies also to whenever hymns are conducted. Try this out on a hymn such as 'Blest are the pure in heart' and see the flow and phrase which automatically comes from thinking of two minims rather than four crotchets in the bar. 'For all the saints' is another hymn which moves more easily at two minims to the bar, and without losing its marching character.

By the reverse token, a hymn such as 'Father, hear the prayer we offer' must have a firm and decisive four beats to the bar. Hymns in triple time are sometimes less easy to think of as one-in-a-bar, though the principle is the same.

To summarize—phrasing adds up to an intelligent approach to any music, and especially to hymnody, if only because of the necessarily four square construction of most hymn tunes.

Variety

In our rightful wish to involve everyone in the singing of hymns, we sometimes make the mistake of expecting everyone to be doing everything all the time. An element of variety not only adds interest but can also help to highlight certain features.

In many situations the farthest we ever get is all voices singing in unison. But need this mean everyone? Verses for men's voices contrast well with women's voices; a verse for boys and girls only is a further variant. While in some churches it is customary for the congregation sometimes to sing a verse on their own, how invaluable it can be for the choir to be given their own verse, in harmony, and preferably unaccompanied.

Everything obviously depends on the available resources. If the congregation consists of five elderly people plus the vicar, any such variation is, of course, virtually non-existent. Given a reasonably sized congregation, a possible way of treating 'Praise to the holiest in the height' might be

verse 1 All voices in unison
verse 2 Harmony
verse 3 Sopranos and trebles
verse 4 Harmony
verse 5 Men's voices in unison
verse 6 Harmony
verse 7 All voices in unison

The use of instruments other than the organ

I can only reiterate here what I have so often said before concerning the galaxy of latent talent in many parishes, much of which is seldom or never tapped.

Instrumental music in many schools is of a high standard and is wide ranging, yet, apart from an annual Christmas carol service or some other special event, how little of this spread of ability finds its way into the regular services of the church? It may be that many of these young instrumentalists are not regular church-goers. If so, what an opportunity exists to invite them in and to involve them by using their special gifts. Enormous pastoral opportunities present themselves to the clergy in this respect.

In some parishes there are families who make music together, sometimes both by singing in the choir and instrumentally. It is always good to see such people involved.

As the use of instruments other than the organ will be dictated by what resources are available to each and every situation, it will probably mean someone with the necessary expertise being prepared to devise and write out the necessary instrumental parts. Alternatively, an existing descant could be used instrumentally instead of vocally.

Where other than traditional hymns are concerned, the music staff of a local school may already have the instrumental parts and therefore be able to help. In the case of existing arrangements, such as Vaughan Williams' so-called Coronation version of *The Old 100th*, parts are available from the publishers, in this instance Oxford University Press.

The piano is a much maligned instrument in terms of the church and is often considered to be unsuitable as compared with the organ. Provided it is of reasonable quality and is regularly tuned and maintained, it can fulfil a valid role, either in its own right or played in conjunction with the organ, the distinctive tone quality of each together providing an ideal and colourful partnership. The percussive quality of the piano and the fact that, being mobile, it can be placed near the singers, makes it ideal and even in some instances superior to the organ. It is also often easier to find a pianist than an organist.

Although these comments are directed towards hymns, they apply equally, and incidentally, to the voluntary, and not least in the contemporary scene to the revival of 'the middle voluntary', which is an ideal opportunity for the contrast provided by the use of instruments other than the organ.

It goes without saying that in those churches where there is no organ the opportunities for using alternative means of hymn accompaniment are wide ranging for those with the vision to grasp the challenge. Of the growing number of churches using instrumental resources, one of the most successful is All Souls, Langham Place, the London church next door to Broadcasting House. Under the guidance and expertise of Noel Tredennick, the visionary organist of the church, a varied and highly effective programme is in operation. From time to time Noel Tredennick conducts RSCM workshops on 'Orchestral Worship', one important feature of which is the orchestration of hymns for whatever resources happen to be available. As an authority on the subject, he will always be glad to give advice and practical help.

Introducing new hymns

Choirs and congregations alike are usually far more receptive to new words than to new tunes, this despite the latter always being the first consideration, misguided though this may be in putting the cart before the horse.

Where new material is concerned, a useful means of preparing the way is for the choir to introduce a new hymn to the congregation a couple of weeks or so before its initial use in a service. If there is no choir, then the organist can play the new tune. It can be a further help if the minister or organist gives a brief verbal explanation about the text and the music as further background information in paving the way as to why a particular hymn is to be introduced. In this way the congregation, many of whom are likely to be conservative in their views and suspicious of anything new in hymnody—or for that matter anything else in church which is new—will at least have had the way prepared for them. The consequent chances are that they will be the more willing to give the new and unfamiliar at least a hearing than if one of their much loved favourites is ousted without so much as a word of explanation. This is surely elementary psychology and a valid way of going about this particular exercise.

It will also be reassuring to hear that a new tune is being introduced as an alternative, and not as a substitute, for an old favourite. 'The King of love my shepherd is' is a familiar example of a hymn where for many years two tunes (*Dominus regit me* and *St Columba*) have been identically associated with, and used for, these words.

Most people are by nature inherently conservative, especially when they get into church. They are therefore by implication suspicious of change, the more so if the way for change is not prepared in advance. This understandably leads to resentment. Even so, having introduced a new tune, it will probably take a number of hearings before being generally accepted. Few new tunes take on overnight, and those that have done so possess certain enduring qualities which make them more or less instant successes. *Abbot's Leigh* (*A and M NSE* 356), *Michael* (*A and M NSE* 336) and *Alberta* (*A and M NSE* 215) are outstanding examples. Others have made their way more slowly, such as *Marching* (*A and M NSE* 113) and *Sine Nomine* (*A and M NSE* 305), which appeared between the wars and which today have with very good reason superseded the tunes by Dykes and Barnby. As neither did much to carry the texts a stage further—the very reverse in fact—this is not all that surprising.

Coda

Two musts for organists and singers:

1. When playing hymns avoid the indiscriminate adding of passing notes, especially the dominant seventh at cadences. The golden rule should always be to play what is in the printed score, although passing notes are *occasionally* to be encouraged. They can all too easily become an irresistible habit, almost to the extent of being a narcotic.

2. Always be aware of rhythmic considerations. Deficiencies in this area show up more in hymns than in any other single aspect of church music, this because of the four-square basic nature of most hymn tunes to which I referred earlier. *Rhythmic consistency and stability must be of the essence.*

   One particular matter which is ignored again and again is the giving of full value to long notes, especially those at the ends of lines, while remembering that time must be allowed for singers to take breath and that this must come out of the long note and *not* in addition to it.

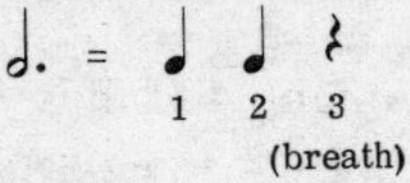

𝅗𝅥. = ♩ ♩ 𝄽
1 2 3
(breath)

(See pages 75 to 77.)

7
SOME INCIDENTALS

Office hymns

It is generally believed that these were introduced by St Ambrose, who lived c. 340–397. Office hymns were intended to be sung at certain stages of the Church's worship. Their use, as their name suggests, was confined to the daily offices of what we now know as Morning and Evening Prayer. Today, as then, they have no place in the Eucharist.

In the course of time they took on quite definite roles in emphasizing the specific seasons of the Church's year, Saints' Days, and the times of the day. Erik Routley defined them more widely when he said that 'the chief end of the office hymn is adoration, and declaration of the divine truth' (*Hymns and Human Life*, page 25, John Murray, 1952).

It was logical to use hymnody to reinforce in song what the spoken word sought to do in other ways. Taken in its broadest context, the concept of the office hymn should underline virtually every occasion when we meet to worship. In practice, although many, if not almost all, hymns in one way or another perform this function, the concept of the office hymn has now been narrowed down to something which is usually a quite simple and homely affair. In the Middle Ages the office hymn was confined to relatively few specific examples such as 'Creator of the earth and sky' (*EH* 49) for use on the Saturday evening from the Octave of the Epiphany till Lent, to 'Now that the daylight fills the sky' for Prime (*EH* 254) and other related examples for Terce, Sext and None, with the familiar 'Before the ending of the day' (*EH* 264) for Compline. A study of

The English Hymnal, which has a full complement of office hymns, will give an insight as to what is available nowadays.

This narrowing down process means that the office hymn is now almost exclusively used at Evensong and sung either to a plainsong tune or otherwise. This will often be determined by the churchmanship concerned, though it is regrettable that plainsong, despite the enlightened age in which we live, is still popularly associated primarily with Anglo-Catholic worship. Ideally, there should be no label attached; the office hymn is there for all of us to use, to enjoy, and to benefit from.

Similarly, although the *EH* and *A and M* examples are specifically marked as office hymns, in practice many churches use a much wider range of material for this purpose. This, although it may have resulted in a much looser definition, has equally resulted in a wider use, which is exactly as it should be. Just as we use Seasonal Sentences and other allied material in ASB Holy Communion Rite A to highlight, emphasize, and make us the more aware of a certain happening, so we should use hymns in a similar way at Evensong.

The precise place at which the office hymn should be sung is speculative. In pre-Reformation times it was clearly specified in the liturgy for use before Magnificat. Percy Dearmer, in his *Short Handbook of Public Worship*, published in 1931, suggested the earlier the better so as to remind people almost at the outset of a service. As it is liturgically incorrect to sing a hymn at the beginning of an office, the earliest feasible moment was before the psalms. Nowadays, the generally agreed place is before Magnificat, though, during my years at Exeter Cathedral we oscillated between the two. Successive clergy tried to convince us with chapter and verse as to the error of our ways, but we eventually settled on the pre-Magnificat position.

In the end, it is all a matter of preference, the main consideration being that we not only know the function of office hymns but that we do in fact use them. Congregations should be aware of their purpose and why we have them.

Hymn festivals

Theoretically, these should be admirable occasions for highlighting the use of hymnody, how to sing hymns to advantage and how to give all concerned insights as to the individual nature and background of each and every example. In practice this proves to be far from easy.

A major limitation is that whereas choirs will come together for a big choral festival which, although it may include hymns, is mainly concerned with the singing of anthems and perhaps canticles, they will far less readily do so, if at all, solely for hymns. The fact that they are consequently missing out on so much which in the right hands of leadership could be to their advantage, is as important a factor as their boycotting such an occasion.

On the other hand, congregations and other local groups are far more ready to join forces to sing hymns, the more so if the lure of television or radio provides an additional bait. While the BBC's weekly *Songs of Praise* has done much over the years to awaken awareness of hymns and hymn singing, the programmes are very variable both in content and performance. In some instances there seems to be a breathless pursuit of fitting as many hymns as possible into the allotted space of time. This can result in hymns losing their dimension and their sense of dignity, especially in large buildings and with larger forces consequently taking part.

A further problem with *Songs of Praise* is the merging of so many styles within one programme. This can range from the traditional to the charismatic chorus and the childrens' song, each with its own characteristic accompaniment. What results is all too often an indigestible conglomeration of bits and pieces which, on balance, tends neither to please nor fulfil many viewers.

Surely one of the best of recent programmes was that from Southwark Cathedral where West Indian choirs and congregation sang with such an uninhibited happiness which came across with great credibility and enjoyment for the viewer. A near runner-up was the programme from Manchester Cathedral which featured school children performing with a high degree of musical perception.

Processions

Worship can be expressed as much by movement and colour as it can be by the use of the voice and instrument. The object and purpose of a procession is that of going somewhere to do something, not merely to arrive at a convenient point, such as walking from the vestry to the choir stalls while singing a hymn. For most general purposes it is far better to process in and out of church to the playing of the organ.

Strictly speaking, the singing of hymns during a procession should only be embarked on at Rogationtide, for the Litany, or at major festivals. On all these occasions it is customary, and correct, to begin at the altar, to end at the altar and to stop at certain places *en route* for prayer. Such is the true ecclesiastical meaning of a station. Obvious stopping places are the crib at Christmas or the Easter garden and font at Easter.

A further symbolic use of the processional hymn is on Advent Sunday to portray the light coming into the world. This is the more meaningful when it is begun in darkness and moves towards the altar as the focal point. In a cathedral this can be even more dramatic if independent choirs can move concurrently from west, south and north singing antiphonally and eventually converging in the sanctuary. In this way the full symbolism of the light coming into the world makes the Advent carol service the more real and meaningful.

On standing for the start of a hymn

Although congregations are quick enough to sit or kneel at the end of a hymn, the business of standing at the beginning is another matter. One of the occupational hazards of church going, which I personally find infuriating, is to see those around me leisurely getting to their feet as and when the spirit moves them, with the stragglers upstanding well after the singing has commenced.

I believe that immediately the organ introduction commences, the entire congregation should stand as one. Most choirs do this but congregations are slow, or loathe, to take this as a cue.

The root of the problem is that whether a hymn is announced or not, many people only start to find that hymn in their books during the organ play-over and are preoccupied with this to the exclusion of all else.

In reality it is all so simple if a congregation is drilled to stand as suggested, either finding the hymn then or, better still, previously. After all, most churches have hymn boards and/or a Sunday bulletin containing this information. I believe that hymns would consequently get off to a much better start if all concerned were on their feet and ready. A valid parallel is surely the start of a race when all concerned are ready in advance and therefore commence as one at the appropriate moment.

In the relatively few churches I know where congregations and choir do stand immediately the organ introduction commences, this simple uniformity of action results in the standard of singing being much higher.

On being fully informed
For all of us concerned in the choice and performance of hymns, there should be the ever mindful need to be well informed, to keep up with current trends and new material and, probably most desirable of all, to be continually looking over our shoulder in a critical way, which not only sees realistically the possible chinks in our armour but also takes every advantage of a shot in the arm.

Reading is one aspect of this, though it needs to be backed up by the enquiring mind which honestly and genuinely wishes to be given new food for thought. Mere lip service will not suffice.

The bibliography at the end of this book can be of help in this respect though, in the end, it is the practical application which really matters. As one example of this I would venture to mention the cassette *Hymns Ancient and Modern 2* which contains eighteen hymns from the two *A and M* supplements, together with some teaching aids and suggestions on performance. This is obtainable from Hymns Ancient and Modern Ltd, St Mary's Works, St Mary's Plain, Norwich NR3 3BH. The object of this cassette is to introduce relatively new material and to do so with an awareness of what underlies the hymns specifically dealt with. I hope that the way in which each hymn is sung and played will provide food for thought which can then be translated, and maybe if necessary adapted, to each and every local scene.

This is but one isolated example of providing help, but it is done with the intention of making people sit up and think more about the whole purpose and performance of hymns. We consequently hope this will help to avoid what can all too easily become something perfunctory and routine. The overall possibilities are considerable and we should be prepared to take advantage of them.

Reiterating four points made earlier

1. I would stress the resultant dangers of choirs and organists relegating, even offloading, hymns as unimportant or unessential. They are crucial and fundamental to virtually every public worship situation.
2. The diversity of gifts to which St Paul alluded suggests that, in terms of hymnody, traditionally trained organists should not be automatically expected to cope with hymns cast in what for many will be something of a foreign mould. I think particularly of the hymns of Beaumont and Appleford and of Sydney Carter.

   It can be equally difficult for those whose expertise lies in this particular field to come to terms with what is required in the performance of traditional hymnody. The two areas of expertise are rarely shared effectively by any one person or group of singers. We should consequently separate the sheep from the goats in order to get the best results in this particular exercise.
3. If you do not already do so, consider sometimes dispensing with a hymn at the offertory and having in its place organ music while the collection is being taken. To sing a doxology such as the last verse of 'Glory to thee, my God, this night' (*A and M NSE* 10), while the offerings are received at the altar, has much to be said in its favour as I have found when in North America.
4. Do campaign for hymns to be sung complete. Where hymns are sung during the communion of the people, nothing is more pernicious and frustrating than having a hymn cut off while it is in full flight simply because the celebrant has finished what he is doing and cannot wait for the hymn to end before getting on with the next part of the service.

I alluded earlier to the fétish for employing hymns as a cover-up for what otherwise would be moments of silence. Quite apart from any other considerations, this is an indefensible and iniquitous way in which to use hymns. The one exception is, of course, the omission of any starred verses which do not destroy the overall sense of the text.

Two further points

1. In the final analysis, never be dull either in the overall conduct of worship or in the music. Being dull, which is too frequently confused somehow with being 'religious', can all too easily be a further occupational hazard of church going.

   The singing of a choir and congregation will be reflected in their looks. I suggest that Jeremy Taylor, the sixteenth century English divine, got it right when he suggested that 'joy is the perfectest convoy for religion'. That just about sums it up.

2. I would reiterate what I said at the outset, namely that this is not intended to be an exhaustive book. It is a general guide for all concerned, much of it born of personal experience, certainly during the past twelve years as a member of the congregation and therefore on the receiving end, instead of being 'up there' in choir and sanctuary as I knew it for so many years.

   This is merely a general guide aimed at picking up the signs of the time, many of which are exciting and challenging, to say the least. But—there are of course danger signs today as at any other time.

8

CODA

Having now come to the end of this particular exercise, it has to be recognized that there is good and bad in every area of hymnody, as there will be in its performance. Where hymns are concerned, the Church has an extraordinary and unfortunate penchant for clinging to the bad, which inevitably includes the sentimental and dated. This applies whether the music is in a traditional mould or otherwise.

On the traditional front there are hymns we ought to be ashamed of perpetrating, both because in an enlightened age we should know better, and because today there is so much alternative–and better–material to choose from. But does taste enter into this? It certainly should.

There are also some distinctly questionable choruses, a lot of froth and bubble with little or no substance or memorability. The repetitive element and the sameness of style verges on boredom. But could not this charge sometimes be laid at the feet of traditional hymnody?

When all the pros and cons are finally weighed up, as they inevitably must be, I am by no means convinced that choruses and related material are necessarily the answer, any more than there is mileage in the altering of texts merely to concede to a fetish concerning sexist language. There will of course be those who will try to convince us otherwise. It is all too fashionable to be 'with it', as those of us subjected to the media know only too well. Any interview situation inevitably becomes channelled in this direction.

Nor does the traditional badly performed necessarily mean that choruses will come off any better.

There always have been, and always will be, things old and things new. There are bad hymns, especially of the nineteenth century. There are also some extremely good ones and the same applies to the hymns of today.

Perhaps the final word should rest with Ralph Vaughan Williams, who reminded us in the music preface to *The English Hymnal* that good taste is 'a moral rather than a musical issue'. But, as Dr Joad would have said, 'It all depends on what you mean by taste'.

A SELECT BIBLIOGRAPHY

A Hymn Book Survey 1962–80, Robin Leaver, Grove Worship Series No. 71.

Hymns with the New Lectionary, compiled by Robin Leaver, Grove Books.

A Hymn Guide for the Sunday Themes of the New Lectionary in The Alternative Service Book 1980, Mowbray, 1981.

These are the Hymns, Alan Dunstan, SPCK, 1973.

Interpreting Worship, Alan Dunstan, Mowbray, 1984.

Hymns and Tunes Indexed by first lines, tune names and metres, David W. Perry, Hymn Society and RSCM, 1980.

The Hymn Explosion, Alan Dunstan, RSCM Handbook No. 6, 1981.

A Handbook of Parish Music, Lionel Dakers, Mowbray, 1976 and 1982.

Church Music in a Changing World, Lionel Dakers, Mowbray, 1984.

Hymns that Live, Frank Colquhoun, Hodder and Stoughton, 1980.

Hymns for Today Discussed, Cyril Taylor, Canterbury Press and RSCM, 1985.

Christian Hymns Observed, Erik Routley, Mowbray, 1983.

The Music of Christian Hymnody, Erik Routley, Independent Press Limited, 1957.

Hymns and Human Life, Erik Routley, Murray, 1952.

News of Hymnody. This quarterly leaflet published by Grove Books, contains reviews, surveys and up to the minute observations on current trends.